Challenges in the Mathematics Education
of African American Children

Proceedings of the Benjamin Banneker Association
Leadership Conference

Edited by

Carol E. Malloy
President, Benjamin Banneker Association
University of North Carolina at Chapel Hill

Laura Brader-Araje
Graduate Student, University of North Carolina at Chapel Hill

National Council of Teachers of Mathematics
Reston, Virginia

Copyright © 1998 by
THE NATIONAL COUNCIL OF TEACHERS OF MATHEMATICS, INC.
1906 Association Drive, Reston, VA 20191-9988
(703) 620-9840; (800) 235-7566; www.nctm.org
All rights reserved

Second printing 2001

Library of Congress Cataloging-in-Publication Data:

Benjamin Banneker Association. Leadership Conference (1997 : Easton, Md.)
    Challenges in the mathematics education of African American children : proceedings of the Benjamin Banneker Association Leadership Conference / edited by Carol E. Malloy, Laura Brader -Araje.
      p.   cm.
    Includes bibliographical references.
    ISBN 0-87353-458-1
    1. Mathematics—Study and teaching—United States—Congresses.
2. Afro-American students—Education—Mathematics—Congresses.
I. Malloy, Carol E.   II. Brader-Araje, Laura.   III. Title.
QA13.B45   1997
510'.71'073—dc21   98-54410
                                                CIP

Funding for the conference was provided by the National Science Foundation.

Printed in the United States of America

Table of Contents

iii

We Are the African-American Children
by Kip Branch

We are the African-American children,
children of the 90s and beyond;

the descendants of all African-American
children who were pulled from their roots
and their mothers' breasts;

we are bright, we are creative, on us rests
the hopes and dreams of a new generation,
one that is striving everywhere;

children whose roots run deep and whose
parents' nurturing and love protect us;

We are the African-American children,
and we move with the visions of our elders,

strong, determined, and enlightened toward
a new and better world.

Foreword

The Benjamin Banneker Association (BBA) is a nonprofit organization of individuals and groups concerned about the mathematics education of African American children. (Throughout this document, we refer to all students of black African heritage who are in the regions served by BBA as African American.) BBA was founded in 1986 to provide a forum for mathematics educators, mathematicians, and other interested people to discuss the learning and teaching of mathematics with respect to African American children. BBA organized this leadership conference to bring together mathematics educators and mathematicians from all sections of the country and the mathematics community to identify issues and generate solutions to meet the challenges associated with the teaching and learning of African American children.

The overriding goal of BBA is to help improve the mathematics education and achievement of African American students. The National Center for Education Statistics reports that in 1994–95 more than 16 percent of school-aged children were African American, and in many urban areas African American and other minority students are between 50 percent and 90 percent of the public school students. National assessment data and state enrollment data indicate that African American children have not reached parity in their opportunities to study and achieve in mathematics. BBA members are deeply committed to identifying and finding solutions to the problems that must be solved in order for parity to be reached.

We realize that leaders in mathematics education must be cognizant of the status of African American students' learning and achievement in mathematics and of research in these areas. They must be familiar with programs that work for African American children, they must be aware of the issues related to policy that affect the learning and teaching of African American children, they must be familiar with innovative curricula developed with every child as the focus, and they must have knowledge about the delivery of appropriate professional development programs and materials. Therefore, the goals of the leadership conference were as follows:

1. To develop a cadre of people who are knowledgeable about the mathematics learning and teaching of African American children and the research in these areas

2. To extend the knowledge of policies that affect the mathematics education of African American children

3. To develop guidelines to assist leaders who will serve as catalysts for change in the mathematics learning of African American children

4. To inform the National Science Foundation and other organizations about issues related to the mathematics education of African American children

The conference was focused through three strands: teaching and learning, policy, and professional development. The learning strand provided information about issues related to the mathematics learning of African American students. The policy strand presented an opportunity for participants to learn about and discuss factors contributing to, and implications of policy decisions on, the mathematics education of African American children. The professional development strand provided participants with information and stimulated discussion to help generate plans for creating written works and professional development activities based on the successful teaching and learning of African American students in mathematics.

Apart from the strands but integral to the process were three presentations on mathematics reform. Reform topics included assessment, NSF-funded curriculum projects, and implementation of the NCTM Standards and other educational reforms in schools within the African American community.

The conference began on Thursday evening, 7 August 1997, and continued through Sunday, 10 August 1997, in Easton, Maryland. The sixty-seven participants and speakers who attended the conference were ethnically, regionally, and professionally diverse. Participants included members of the BBA Board of Directors; teachers from elementary, middle, and high schools; mathematics educators; mathematicians; mathematics supervisors; and presidents from national mathematics education organizations. Because the conference was limited to sixty-seven participants, active members had to apply to attend the conference and were selected by BBA regional representatives. The invitations were based on members' participation in recent professional development activities, their attendance at recent state or local professional meetings, and their commitment to actively carrying out the goals of the conference in their geographical region. Participants also agreed to plan and lead regional meetings and implement school-based initiatives that evolved from the conference.

The Benjamin Banneker Association sincerely thanks Alverna Champion for her encouragement and support as the association planned and implemented this conference.

The conference committee members, Donald Bradford, Beatrice Moore-Harris, Carol Malloy, William Tate, and Irvin Vance, planned a meeting where mathematics educators could speak to, listen to, and learn from one another. We identified issues and generated solutions to help meet the challenges associated with the teaching and learning of African American children. Six speakers were commissioned to develop papers that addressed the conference strands. Their presented papers, along with summaries of discussions and individual papers, are included in this book. The discussion summaries reflect the thoughts, ideas, and recommendations of the participants. We hope that the reader can use the knowledge and recommendations in this book to help formulate plans to strengthen the mathematics teaching and learning of African American children, with the understanding that educational programs that strengthen the learning of African American children will ultimately serve *all* children.

Carol E. Malloy
Conference Chair and President
Benjamin Banneker Association

Agenda

Challenges in the Mathematics Education of African American Children
Benjamin Banneker Association Leadership Conference

Thursday, 7 August 1997

6:00 P.M.   Reception Sponsored by Texas Instruments
7:00 P.M.   Dinner

Keynote Speaker
Gloria Ladson-Billings, University of Wisconsin—Madison
It Doesn't Add Up: African American Students' Mathematics Achievement

Friday, 8 August 1997

8:30 A.M.–9:15 A.M.

Opening Comments, *Carol E. Malloy, President, Benjamin Banneker Association*
Greetings, *Margaret B. Cozzens, National Science Foundation*

9:30 A.M.–11:00 A.M.

Strand: African American Learning
Breakout Sessions
Guiding Questions

1. What activities should BBA be sponsoring with respect to African American student learning?

2. What pedagogy and materials are appropriate to help African American children be successful in mathematics learning?

3. How do we use the cultural strengths of African American children in mathematics instruction?

4. What unique characteristics and factors are there about African American children and their culture that contribute to the struggle and stigma surrounding them and their mathematical learning?

5. How are African American children who have superior aptitude for mathematics identified, encouraged, and challenged in a political climate that advocates heterogeneous grouping and collaborative or cooperative instructional strategies?

6. What are the implications of the implementation of constructivist learning theory and collaboration on the learning of African American children?

7. What can educators do to motivate and turn around students who have low self-esteem and have become complacent with being mathematical failures? How can we stimulate students and develop persistence?

8. What role should technology play in the learning of African American children?

11:15 A.M.–12:00 Noon   Reporting and Conclusions

1:30 P.M.–3:00 P.M.

Strand: Mathematics Education Reform
Assessment, Evaluation, Mathematics Education Reform, and African American Students: A Framework
Frank E. Davis, Lesley College
NSF Curriculum Projects
Glenda Lappan, President-Elect, National Council of Teachers of Mathematics; Michigan State University

3:30 P.M.–4:00 P.M.

Charge to Regional Caucus Teams
Carol E. Malloy, President Benjamin Banneker Association,
University of North Carolina at Chapel Hill

4:15 P.M.–5:30 P.M.   Regional Caucuses

7:30 P.M.–9:00 P.M.   BBA Board Meeting

Saturday, 9 August 1997
9:00 A.M.–9:45 A.M.

Strand: Policy
The Politics of Urban Mathematics Education
Stephen R. Cox, Temple University

10:00 A.M.–11:30 A.M.

Breakout Sessions
Guiding Questions

1. What should BBA be doing with respect to policies that influence African American student achievement?

2. How can we ensure that a standards-based education is being implemented fairly for all students?

3. What can be done with respect to <u>standardized</u> testing (e.g, statewide proficiency tests) to guarantee that <u>all</u> students, especially African Americans, have an equal opportunity to succeed?

4. What are the pros and cons about a national assessment? What are the implications of the new eighth-grade (voluntary) test on African American children, teachers, and their communities?

5. How can we guarantee that all students will have access to technology in teaching and learning, regardless of socioeconomic levels?

6. What state, district, school, and classroom policies impede the mathematics progress of African American children at the elementary, middle, and secondary school levels? What actions should BBA take with respect to these policies?

11:45 A.M.–12:30 P.M.   Reporting and Conclusions

2:00 P.M.–2:45 P.M.

Strand: Professional Development
Professional Development for Urban School Districts
Marieta W. Harris, Memphis City Schools

3:00 P.M.–4:30 P.M.

Breakout Sessions
Guiding Questions

1. What should BBA be doing with respect to professional development for teachers of African American children?

2. How do we create an Afrocentric mathematics curriculum?

3. How do we develop the usefulness of mathematics that is proactive and progressive enough to teach our African American children to understand the necessity to free themselves from control and protect themselves from economic exploitation?

4. How do we address the "basic skills" versus "constructing understanding" dichotomy as it relates to the education of African American children?

5. What are the essential things teachers need to know about African American children before they begin to teach them mathematics?

6. What strategies are necessary and how do we help teachers enhance the levels of African American student discourse about mathematical ideas?

7. What are worthwhile mathematical tasks, and how do we help teachers to recognize these tasks and use them in their instruction?

8. How do teachers move to a no-fault system of education where parents, prior teachers, and the students themselves are not blamed or considered the excuse for lack of knowledge? How do we start teaching where the students are?

4:45 P.M.–5:30 P.M.   Reporting and Conclusions
7:30 P.M.–9:00 P.M.   Regional Caucuses

Sunday, 10 August 1997

8:30 A.M.–9:15 A.M.

Strand: Mathematics Education Reform
When the Vision Confronts Reality:
Implementing Reform in Elementary School Mathematics in an Urban School District
Patricia F. Campbell, University of Maryland

9:30 A.M.–10:45 A.M.   Regional Caucuses
11:00 A.M.–12:00 Noon

Challenges and Charge to the Benjamin Banneker Association
Edgar Edwards, BBA Founding Member

Opening Comments

Charge to Mathematics Educators:
What We Want in Mathematics Classrooms

Margaret B. Cozzens
National Science Foundation

As a research mathematician who has spent the past six years at the National Science Foundation (NSF) working to improve mathematics and science education in our grades K–12 schools nationwide, I was surprised to read in *the New York Times* and the *Wall Street Journal* that, in some quarters, the National Council of Teachers of Mathematics (NCTM) Standards are being disparaged as "fuzzy math" and the antithesis of clear thinking (Lynne Cheney, "Creative Math, or Just Fuzzy Math?", *New York Times*, 11 August 1997; "President Clinton's Mandate for Fuzzy Math," *Wall Street Journal*, 11 June 1997). The tone of these pieces, and some of their inaccuracies, demonstrate the need to clarify what the Standards are and are not.

But first, I should note that as a nation, we should be heartened by the recent strong showing made by U.S. fourth graders on the Third International Mathematics and Science Study (TIMSS). Though not yet "first in the world," we are gaining rapidly. The most comprehensive international assessment of its kind to date, TIMSS shows that U.S. nine-year-olds are grouped in a small cohort of nations ranked second in the world in science and sixth in the world in mathematics. TIMSS also shows dramatic improvement in U.S. elementary school students' mathematics achievement since the last international test in 1991.

But neither I nor many of my colleagues find these results surprising. The U.S. ranking is a direct result of changes in mathematics and science education that began in 1989, with the release of the NCTM *Curriculum and Evaluation Standards for School Mathematics*. These changes continue today at NSF and elsewhere with the development of instructional materials and teacher professional development programs based on the *Standards*. It is true that the *Standards* documents contain no specific curricula, instructional materials, examples of classroom practice, or assessments. That is because they are not intended to. But they do provide a solid framework for schools and teachers of what children should know and be able to do in mathematics at various grade levels.

The *Standards* documents emphasize the need for students to master early the basic skills of addition, subtraction, multiplication, and division. The *Standards* differ from "traditional" curricula because they also insist that students should not be limited to learning only those "basic skills." What the *Standards* require is that all our children, not just those labeled the "best and brightest," should be provided with the opportunity to learn mathematics—as opposed to solely rote arithmetic—so that they will be able to apply what they've learned to solve problems they might well encounter in the world outside the classroom and gain an understanding of mathematics that survives after graduation, something that rote learning generally has not yet succeeded in doing.

The *Standards* do encourage the use of calculators and computers, but not as a substitute for learning. Just as many of us balance our checkbooks by hand and use a calculator to check our work, so too can students use a calculator to check their work. Professional statisticians once computed such complex variables as coefficients of correlation by hand; none would do so today. The use of calculators requires a strong grasp of the "basics" in order to estimate a correct answer and verify whether an answer is reasonable. Skilled teachers know when to use calculators in classrooms and when not to; no one advocates the use of calculators to the exclusion of other methods.

But computation, although important, is only one aspect of mathematics. The real challenge in teaching meaningful mathematics is to provide students with enough knowledge and skill to enable them to reason, solve problems, and communicate their solutions to others. Mathematicians think about a problem, devise partial solutions, talk with their colleagues, work some more, talk some more, and finally finish the solution and share it with others to be critiqued. This is collaborative work at its best, but in no way does it discount the individual who eventually solves the problem. In U.S. schools, mathematics too often is synonymous with memorization rather than thinking. We know from research that collaborative learning is one way of encouraging the active learning of all students. We know from business and industry that people need to be able to work in groups, share ideas, challenge one another, and build on one another's work.

The *Standards* attempt to emulate this approach in the classroom. Part of the criticism of the *Standards*, I believe, stems from the reality that adults tend to believe—whether they ought to or not, and no matter how long ago they finished school—that the way they were taught is the "right way" to learn. However, William Schmidt, an NSF-funded TIMSS researcher at Michigan State University who has compared eighth-grade curricula in the United States and abroad, points out that what makes the U.S. middle schools inferior to those of high-scoring nations is not that U.S. schools give short shrift to the basic computational skills, but that what other countries consider "basic learning" involves far more than just elementary computation. Eighth graders in Japan, Korea, and Singapore are studying elements of geometry and algebra, whereas their counterparts in the United States often don't get beyond basic arithmetic because the existing U.S. curriculum stresses endless repetition of these skills. Since the NCTM Standards have begun to be adopted in U.S. schools, elementary school mathematics lessons have begun to approximate more closely not only the methods of mathematicians but also the ways in which high-performing nations teach mathematics.

Meanwhile, we need to take note of something even more important: although U.S. fourth graders did well on TIMSS, there is a marked drop-off in students' performance on TIMSS at the eighth-grade level. This dramatic difference in performance should tell us two things. First, *Standards*-based teaching has begun to make a difference in elementary school achievement scores, which we see in the improved scores since 1991. Second, we now need to concentrate on vigorous implementation of quality mathematics instruction in middle schools because too few school systems have done that. Implementing quality mathematics instruction means providing (1) quality professional development opportunities for teachers to use these *Standards*-based materials and (2) the administrative support necessary to create a learning community among the teachers.

Learning mathematics to high standards by eighth grade is hard. So is teaching to achieve those standards. Our teachers and students will need help to ensure success for all students. Rather than arguing about which approach to teaching mathematics is better or about the value of the NCTM Standards, members of the public, especially those who see the value in competency in mathematics and the need for this competency among all our citizens, should come out forcefully in support of *Standards*-based mathematics teaching and learning for all. The Banneker Association should be outspoken in encouraging a dialogue that helps all our children learn mathematics that goes beyond simple arithmetic skills.

There is nothing fuzzy about mathematics that goes beyond computation, since the whole body of mathematical knowledge and research has gone far beyond simple calculations. I, for one, would never have earned a doctorate in mathematics if mathematics had been restricted to learning computational algorithms like adding, subtracting, multiplying, and dividing. I suffered through a school mathematics program that overused worksheets consisting of hundreds of "basic" problems, one just like the next and like the one before it. I do not want that system for my grandchildren.

NSF is committed to funding the development of *Standards*-based instructional materials, curricula, and teacher professional development programs so that local school districts can help each of their students to become successful in mathematics and, more important, to retain what they have learned so they can use it in their everyday lives. NSF needs those committed to these goals.

Presentations

It Doesn't Add Up: African American Students' Mathematics Achievement

Gloria Ladson-Billings
University of Wisconsin—Madison

Mathematics education has been heralded for its leadership role in the U.S. school reform effort (Stein, Grover, and Henningsen 1996; Grant, Peterson, and Shojgreen-Downer 1996). Prominent in the reform of mathematics education is the call for students not merely to memorize formulas and rules and apply procedures but rather to engage in the *processes* of mathematical thinking, that is, to do what mathematicians and other professional users of mathematics do. The revamped mathematics education program is based on engaging students in problem posing and problem solving rather than on rote memorization and convergent thinking. These changes in mathematics education suggest that mathematics teaching must build on students' learning and ability to pose and solve problems previously considered too difficult for their age-grade levels (Carpenter and Fennema 1988; Fennema et al. 1993).

Despite the much talked about changes in mathematics education, African American students continue to perform poorly in school mathematics (Secada 1992). Some have argued that African American children's poor mathematics performance is the result of a discontinuity that exists between students' home language and the perceived "precision" of mathematics and mathematical language (Orr 1987). Others have suggested that the content of school mathematics is so divorced from students' everyday experiences that it appears irrelevant (Tate 1994). However, few have situated the mathematics performance of African American students in the larger context of mathematics teaching and learning in U.S. schools. This discussion attempts to do just that and suggests some direction for further research on the mathematics performance of African American students.

Why African Americans?

Some may ask, why the focus on African American students? However, the telling statistics on the life chances of African Americans suggest that whenever we can improve the schooling experiences for African American students, we have an opportunity to reverse those life chances. A disturbing percentage of African American males are involved with the criminal justice system (Miller 1997). There are more African American males in jail than in college. Today, for the first time in our history, there are more African American males in jail than whites males (Miller 1997). African American students are two to five times more likely to be suspended (and at a younger age) than white students (Carnegie Corporation of New York 1984/85). The dropout rate for urban, inner-city African American youth is 36 percent and rising (Whitaker 1988). And although graduation from high school is no guarantee of success in life, a life without a high school diploma is almost certain to be unsuccessful—economically and socially.

In the 1950s and 1960s, civil rights leaders declared literacy to be the key to full citizenship for African Americans (Morris 1984). If African Americans could become literate, they could not be denied the franchise in those southern states that had imposed literacy tests as a condition for voting. They could begin to read and discern for themselves the political practices that could lead to liberation. Much like the work of Paulo Freire (1970), these efforts toward increased literacy for African Americans were infused with notions of developing "critical consciousness," or an ability to read both the world and the word.

Today, in the 1990s, one of the stalwarts of the civil rights movement, Bob Moses, has argued that mathematical literacy represents the "new" civil rights battleground (Jetter 1993). Moses asserts that because of the critical role of algebra as a curricular gatekeeper, urban students cannot continue to be tracked out of it, that is, in the current arrangement of the curriculum, access to higher-level mathematics beginning with algebra can mean increased educational and economic opportunities for students.

The Culture of America and the Culture of Mathematics

Although this discussion is focused on African American students' mathematics achievement, it is important to situate it in the larger context of mathematics teaching and learning in America. The Third International Mathematics and Science Study (TIMSS) (U.S. Department of Education 1996) revealed that American schoolchildren continue to lag behind students in other highly technological nations in mathematics and science achievement. The reasons for these lags are multiple—teachers without adequate mathematics and science preparation, unimaginative approaches to teaching, teacher misassignment, poorly constructed texts. But it is more than what happens in our classrooms that contributes to the creation of a mathematically illiterate culture. Mathematics functions as a "feared/revered" subject in our culture. We fear it because we believe that it is "too hard," and we revere it because we believe it signals advanced thinking reserved only for the intelligentsia.

Ours is a nation where no one would readily admit to being unable to read but many proclaim with pride their inability to balance their checkbooks or compute the amount of interest on a loan. Not knowing how to read or write carries a stigma across race, class, and gender lines. People who cannot read and write attempt to mask that fact by using a variety of strategies. They pretend that they cannot see without their eyeglasses. They rely on their memories to pretend to read what they have heard many times before, or they grasp at context clues to make meaning from the meaningless squiggles on signs and paper.

Contrast this behavior with that of people in our society who struggle with mathematics. As Stevenson (1992) reported, whereas Asian parents attributed their students' mathematics failure to lack of effort, U.S. parents were more likely to suggest that their children's poor mathematics performance was attributable to a lack of innate ability. In the United States there is a cultural belief that either one "has it" or does not when it comes to mathematical ability and that the way to "get it" is through genetic inheritance.

As previously stated, it is more acceptable in our society to be mathematically inept. Although hardly anyone will admit to being unable to read and write, Americans often matter of factly comment on their limited mathematics skills. Mathematical ability has come to be associated with "nerdiness" or "geekiness." Our cultural portrayals of the mathematically adept are white males with horn-rimmed glasses and plastic pocket protectors. These images do not prompt our children to embrace mathematics as a field of study or a necessary skill. This distortion and mystification of mathematics and its uses has contributed to our positioning it as unattainable and undesirable.

We also have to understand that as our economy has changed from one where a high school education and a work ethic could allow one to find reasonable employment and provide for oneself and one's family to a more bifurcated one where people either are highly educated (or skilled) or poorly educated (and unskilled), the role of mathematics (and science) teachers has changed. In the earlier era, mathematics teachers were charged with using their subject area as a curriculum sieve, that is, sifting and winnowing to select out the top students to go on to higher mathematics. In our current highly technological, global economy, few Americans can afford to be left out of high-level mathematics. Thus, today's mathematics teachers must conceive of their subject area not as a sieve but as a net that gathers in more and more students. This paradigmatic shift has been a difficult one for our students as a whole, but it has been particularly difficult for African American students.

But some people do well in mathematics in our society. Why? There are certainly individual differences that cannot be easily generalized to explain mathematical abilities. However, statistically we can see whole-group patterns that may suggest some tendencies. White middle-class male students (as well as some groups of students of Asian descent) typically do well in mathematics. Is there anything about the culture of mathematics that is compatible with white middle-class male students' and Asians' culture and experiences? Is there anything about white middle-class male students' and Asians' culture that makes it compatible with mathematics as it is taught in our schools?

Mathematics teaching in our schools emphasizes repetition; drill; convergent, right-answer thinking; and predictability. (This description of current mathematics practice does not reflect those school programs that have adopted the recommended NCTM *Standards*.) Students are asked to perform similar tasks over and over. They rarely are asked to *challenge* the ways that "rules" of mathematics might be *challenged*. They rarely are asked how their prior knowledge and experience might support or conflict with school mathematics. The demands of middle-class culture are for efficiency, consensus, abstraction, and rationality. There is nothing inherently good or bad about these features of the culture. However, they may reflect the experiences and understandings of one segment of our society. (Although no one monolithic African American culture exists, scholars such as Nobles [1986] and Boykin and Toms [1985] have identified features extant in African American cultural expression that appear with regularity throughout African American communities.) Boykin and Toms (1985) suggest that some features of African American cultural expression include rhythm, orality, communalism, spirituality, expressive individualism, perspective of social time, verve, and movement. Once again, there is nothing inherently good or bad about these cultural features. However, these kinds of cultural expression are not reinforced or represented in school mathematics. An example of the different ways white and African American students may think about mathematical problem solving was evident in some pilot studies of curriculum reform (Tate 1994).

Researchers presented students in a white middle-class suburban community and an African American urban community with the following problem:

> It costs one dollar each way to ride the metropolitan bus. The cost of a monthly "fast pass" is $50. Which is more economical for commuting to and from work?

Students were encouraged to raise questions about the problem before coming up with a solution. The white suburban middle-class students had no questions. Instead, they quickly set about doing the computation to solve the problem. They figured a five-day work week in a thirty-day month, minus four weekends, or eight nonwork days, equaled twenty-two days multiplied by two dollars a day. Their answer of $44 was $6 cheaper than the $50 "fast pass," and thus the students concluded that the "logical" choice was to pay the one-dollar fare each way.

The African American urban students took a different tack. They followed through on the researchers' request that they pose questions about the problem. One of the first questions they asked was, "How many jobs are we talking about?" Because of their experience with adults who have more than one job, the students could envision a worker who went to work in the morning, got off in the evening, went to a second job, and came home late at night. This worker would need three fares instead of the two imagined by the white students. The students also asked questions about whether or not the worker owned a car. If not, the worker would use public transportation for more than going to work. She or he might use it on the weekend to go shopping, to attend church, visit friends, or go out for entertainment. The students asked how many people were in the imagined family. This question spoke to the students' understanding that a "fast pass" was transferable and a variety of people could use it at different times. Finally, the students posed an ethical question. Why would the bus company constantly advertise the savings to be realized by a "fast pass" if it were indeed cheaper to pay the dollar fare?

The contrast in the students' responses represent their very different life experiences and approaches to problem solving. For the white students the problem was "outside" of their experiences. They lacked the kind of experiences that would allow them to ask relevant questions. They made sense of it as an abstraction. The problem had little meaning, but they knew enough arithmetic to manipulate the numbers. The African American students, when encouraged to seriously consider the problem, *situated it in their own social contexts*. Bus riding was something they knew about, and they willingly demonstrated their expertise.

Beyond Surface Differences

But it is not merely students' social context that affects students' mathematics achievement. The relationship between mathematics and culture continues to be deciphered. There are those who will suggest that mathematics is "culture-free" and it does not matter who is "doing" mathematics; the tasks remain the same. But these are people who do not understand the nature of culture and its profound impact on cognition (Cole et al. 1971).

Culture refers to the deep structures of knowing, understanding, acting, and being in the world. It is the basis for all human thought and activity and cannot be suspended as human beings interact with particular subject matters or domains of learning. Its transmission is both explicit and implicit. Thus, even though African American students are a part of almost every social strata and their social context may influence what experiences they have and how they view the world, their cultural knowledge, expressions, and understandings, which may be transmitted over many generations, may share many features with African Americans across socioeconomic and geographical boundaries.

Part of the deep structure of African American culture is an affinity for rhythm and pattern. (It is important that this sentence not be read as the stereotypical "all black people got rhythm." Instead, I suggest that rhythmic expressions in music, dance, art, etc., consistently are valued and reinforced in African American cultural expression. Individuals within the culture may have no particularly rhythmic skills or interests.) African American artistic and physical expressions demonstrate these features in sophisticated ways. Jazz, gospel music, rap, poetry, basketball, sermonizing, dance, fashion, all reflect African American influences of rhythm and pattern. But these influences rarely are connected to any mathematical foundations. I am not suggesting that we should "mathematize"—a term used to explain the practice of quantifying nonmathematical phenomena; see Putnam, Lampert, and Peterson (1990)—all cultural expressions such as art and music, but rather it may be important to help students see the mathematical links that exist between what they know and appreciate.

School mathematics is presented in ways that are divorced from the everyday experiences of most students, not just African American students. Thus, poor mathematics performance in the United States cuts across cultural groups. But there are some disturbing patterns about the performance of African American students that need to be questioned. Jeannie Oakes and her colleagues (1990) found that low-income African American students are more likely to be clustered in low-ability mathematics classes. As African American enrollment increases, the proportion of classes identified as "high ability" diminishes. Schools where African American students constitute the majority have less extensive and less demanding mathematics programs and have fewer opportunities to take "gatekeeper" courses such as algebra and calculus that lead to increased opportunities at the college level and beyond. Oakes and her colleagues also found that schools with high concentrations of African American students tended to have fewer teachers judged to be highly qualified in mathematics.

Teaching for High Performance in Mathematics

Although much of this discussion has dealt with the way mathematics is constructed and regarded in the United States, I would be remiss if I did not address the notion of pedagogy, for it is within changed notions of pedagogy that I believe we have the best opportunity for changing the achievement levels of African American students. My work has focused on successful teachers of African American students (e.g., Ladson-Billings [1994, 1995]). The work of such teachers is in high relief from that of what Haberman (1991) calls "the pedagogy of poverty." This pedagogy of poverty includes routine teaching acts such as "giving information, asking questions, giving directions, making assignments, monitoring seatwork, reviewing assignments, giving tests, reviewing tests, assigning homework, reviewing homework, settling disputes, punishing noncompliance, marking papers, and giving grades" (p. 290). Haberman points out that taken separately, these acts might seem "normal." However, "taken together and performed to the systematic exclusion of other acts, they have become the pedagogical coin of the realm in urban schools" (p. 291).

Furthermore, Haberman suggests that the pedagogy of poverty appeals to several constituencies (p. 291). The following are some connections to mathematics teaching and learning based on Haberman's work:

- *It appeals to those who themselves did not do well in school.* Too many of the teachers assigned to urban classrooms fail to enjoy intellectual pursuits. Their own work in school was mediocre, and teaching was a choice of convenience rather than one of informed and reflective decision making. These teachers typically were not good mathematics students, and their orientation to mathematics is as a rule-governed, right-answer, "hard" discipline.

- *It appeals to those who rely on common sense rather than on thoughtful analysis.* Teachers who practice this kind of pedagogy are more likely to suggest that students need to learn or do something because that is the way they learned or did it. Rather than make curricular and instructional decisions that are based on empirical research or a systematic study of students' classroom performances, they do what "feels" right. Thus, strictly following the mathematics text and completing problem sets become the rule.

- *It appeals to those who fear people of color and the poor (and have a need for control).* It is interesting to walk into schools or classrooms thought to be "good" urban classrooms. Often, what makes them "good" is that they are unnaturally quiet. Teachers and administrators sometimes become so consumed with the notion that African American children must be "managed" that they forget that they need to be taught. Maintaining order and keeping children under control become the preoccupation of the teachers Haberman describes. Order may be best maintained by giving students mundane, routine mathematics tasks that do not invite much discussion and challenge.

- *It appeals to those who have low expectations for children of color and the poor.* As was previously mentioned, there is a prevailing notion in American culture that academic excellence is a result of genetic good fortune. This concept that some students "have it" whereas others do not is particularly pernicious when directed toward African American students. Teachers who presume that because students are of a particular race or ethnicity they cannot be expected to perform at high levels in mathematics fail to present those students with a challenging, intellectually rigorous mathematics curriculum. Instead, their mathematics curriculum is best described as overly directive and controlling.

- *It appeals to those who do not know the full range of available pedagogical options.* It stands to reason that if teachers haven't performed well in school, approach teaching unsystematically, fear their students, and hold low expectations for them, they are likely also to possess a limited teaching repertoire. Calling on past (bad) practices, these teachers tend to reproduce the kind of unimaginative, stifling pedagogy that has failed to serve students of color for many years. Their classrooms are not unlike that described by Ayers (1992, p. 259):

> Visiting a fourth grade class, I was greeted by the teacher. "Welcome to our class," she said. "I'm on page 307 of the math text, exactly where I'm supposed to be according to board guidelines."
>
> There was not much going on—two students were asleep, several were looking out the window, a few were reading their math books. I discovered later that virtually every student in the class was failing math. But this teacher was doing her job, moving through the set curriculum, dutifully delivering the material, passing out the grades. If the students did not learn math, that was not her responsibility.

In contrast to this pedagogy of poverty, I have had the pleasure of working with teachers who enacted a culturally relevant pedagogy. I have documented their work in a number of places (Ladson-Billings 1994, 1995). However, in keeping with an emphasis on mathematics, I want to discuss the way one of the teachers, whom I call Margaret, developed a pedagogy designed to ensure high mathematical achievement among African American students.

Margaret is an Italian American woman in her middle forties. She began her teaching career in the late 1960s as a Dominican nun. She has taught students in both private and public schools from white wealthy communities to low-income communities of color. When the study was done, she was teaching sixth grade in a working-class, low-income, predominantly African American school district. Although regarded as a "strict" teacher, she knew that students respected her for being a demanding, yet caring teacher.

Mathematics in Margaret's class was a nonstop affair. She spent little or no time on classroom routines like taking roll, collecting lunch money, or classroom management. Margaret's classroom was always busy. Although they were engaged in problem solving using algebraic functions, no worksheets were handed out, no problem sets were assigned. The students, as well as Margaret, posed problems.

From a pedagogical standpoint, I saw Margaret make a point of getting every student involved in the mathematics lesson. She continually assured students that they were capable of mastering the problems. They cheered each other on and celebrated when they were able to explain how they arrived at their solutions. Margaret's time and energy were devoted to mathematics.

Margaret moved around the classroom as students posed questions and suggested solutions. She often asked, "How do you know?" to push students' thinking. When students asked questions, Margaret was quick to say, "Who knows? Who can help him out here?" Margaret helped her students understand that they were knowledgeable and capable of answering questions posed by themselves and others. However, Margaret did not shrink from her own responsibility as teacher. From time to time she worked individually with students who seemed puzzled or confused about the discussion. By asking a series of probing questions, Margaret was able to help students organize their thinking about a problem and develop their own problem-solving strategies. The busy hum of activity in Margaret's classroom was directed toward mathematics.

All Margaret's students participated in algebra, even though it was beyond what the district's curriculum required for sixth grade. Margaret scrounged an old set of algebra books from the district's book closet and exempted no one from the rigors of the class. One of her students was designated a "special needs" student. However, Margaret determined that with a few accommodations the student could remain in the classroom and benefit from her instruction. "James" performed well in the classroom. He participated in class discussions, posed problems as well as solved them, and accepted help from classmates when he struggled. By the end of the year, Margaret had convinced the principal that there was no need for James to receive services outside the classroom.

Although it is interesting to hear Margaret's story, it is more meaningful to understand her practice as a heuristic for

solving the problem of poor mathematics achievement among African American students. Some of the tentative principles we can extrapolate from her teaching include the following:

1. *Students treated as competent are likely to demonstrate competence.* Much of the literature on teachers' expectations of students' achievement helps us understand that when teachers believe in their students' abilities, the students are likely to be successful. Conversely, when teachers believe that students, either because of their race, social class, or personal economic situations, may not be intellectually able, the students' performance (and how it is assessed) confirms those beliefs. Margaret treated all her students as if they were intellectually exceptional. She expected all her students to perform at high levels of competence—and they did.

2. *Providing instructional scaffolding for students allows them to move from what they know to what they do not know.* Rather than worry about what students do not know, Margaret demonstrated that it is possible to use the students' prior knowledge as a bridge to new learning. She instructed her students not to allow the test's or text's organization to distract or confuse them. She reassured them that they possessed strategies for solving a variety of problems.

3. *The major focus of the classroom must be instructional.* Margaret made efficient use of her class time. From the moment the students entered the classroom until the time they were dismissed for recess, they were engaged in mathematics. Additionally, Margaret was engaged in *mathematics instruction* the entire time. She did not attempt to occupy the students with "busy work." Instead, she was committed to the academic success of each of the students and accompanied them on the instructional journey. Knowing that she was right there with them, she assured the students that their progress would be monitored and that they would never be allowed to stray too far off the instructional path.

4. *Real education is about extending students' thinking and abilities beyond what they already know.* Margaret's decision to teach her sixth graders algebra even when it was not mandated by her district's curriculum was a conscious decision to demonstrate to the students that they had the capacity to learn and perform at higher and more sophisticated levels than had been demanded of them previously. Instead of attempting to maintain the students at low levels of academic performance, Margaret presented challenging content for *all* the students.

5. *Effective pedagogical practice involves in-depth knowledge of students as well as subject matter.* There is no disputing that effective teachers must be knowledgeable about content. Additionally, Shulman (1987) suggests that beyond knowledge of their various content areas,

teachers must know how that knowledge is best taught. Other researchers argue that teachers who are successful with diverse learners also are able to cultivate and maintain strong interpersonal relationships with their students (Foster 1992).

Spindler (1982) reports that teachers, perhaps unconsciously, favor those students whom they perceive to be most like them. This favoring takes the form of attending more to these students, valuing their responses more, and evaluating their performances more favorably. If teachers are to be more effective with African American students, they must develop a positive identification with them—to perceive African Americans to be like them, fully human and possessed of enormous intellectual capacity.

Filling the Research Void— "Complex Situations"

One of the ways researchers might begin to develop research agendas that respond to the needs of classroom teachers and their students to improve mathematics performance is to understand the theoretical challenge of this work. A typical response to these issues is to function in a "crisis management" mode—looking for ways to repair seemingly irreparable classroom situations. I want to suggest here that a better way to address these problems is to develop more-powerful theoretical rubrics for making sense of classroom practices and student performances. Two important heuristics for creating a "way of seeing" what is happening in mathematics classrooms are found in the work of Lave and Wenger (1991) and Waldrop (1992). The former gives us an understanding of the situated nature of learning, or *situated* cognition. The latter helps us develop notions of *complexity*. Together, they might be thought of as a theory of "complex situations."

Situated cognition suggests that individuals do not learn things in a vacuum. Rather, learning occurs in social contexts. The kinds of mathematics learning that individuals do can be highly specific. Fasheh (1990) speaks of his mother's understanding of pattern because of her work as a quilter. Similarly, when teaching adults to read in the South during the 1950s and 1960s, Septima Clark (1990) relied primarily on her students' desire to gain employment, read and study the Bible, and participate in the political process as sources of reading motivation instead of trying to teach rudiments of sound-symbol relationships. Thus, success in mathematics for African American students may need to be deeply embedded in their everyday contexts. Instead of surface connections, such as changing the names of story problem characters, teachers will need to understand the deep structures of students' experiences. (Knowing these deep structures goes beyond reading general descriptions of a culture to becoming a "student" of the specific individuals we teach.) This may mean doing some things with students that look very "unmathlike"—interviewing them, having them write auto-biographies, discussing interests. To be successful at moving from students' lives and interests to meaningful mathematics, teachers themselves will have to be very knowledgeable in mathematics. The work of Smith and Stiff (1993) illustrates this technique. Under the press of a state mandate for algebra for all students, Smith and Stiff created a series of vignettes tied to students' interests in which they embedded the basics of algebra. Their technique involved students in these high-interest stories until students' interest waned. When the interest dissipated, a new story was begun. Students' ability to move from story to story was tied to their knowledge of mathematics. They could (and did) embed the algebraic concepts and problems in any story. However, it was the interest in the story that kept the students engaged. This technique is important in light of the push to create high-technology programs for mathematics learning. These programs necessarily must choose some context, but they may not choose the "right" contexts. (For example, my middle school daughter's mathematics class participated in the highly acclaimed Jasper Woodbury Series, created as a part of Vanderbilt University's School for Thought program. Although she completed the assignments, throughout the study she complained that she was not particularly interested in Jasper and his problems. The Smith and Stiff project requires that the problems emanate from students in the classroom.)

In addition to situating the teaching of mathematics in relevant student contexts, we need to recognize that human contexts or systems are necessarily complex. Casti (1994) and Waldrop (1992), constructors of "complexity theory," suggest that phenomena (or tasks) are not just "complicated," they are "complex." The classroom *is* a complicated place. But complicated phenomena and tasks typically can be reduced to the sum of their parts, whereas complex systems such as human beings, communities, schools, and classrooms are "more dynamic, more unpredictable, more alive" (Davis and Sumara 1997, p. 117). Thus, classrooms are *both* complicated and complex.

Waldrop (1992) asserts that complex systems have three distinguishing characteristics. First, they have the capacity to undergo spontaneous self-organization, somehow managing to transcend themselves in the process. For example, in the process of solving a mathematics problem, individual students might contribute different ideas that help create a rubric or strategy for solving the problem that no one student would have developed independently. Second, complex systems are adaptive. Whether they be species, marketplaces, or individual organisms (or classrooms), they all change within changing environments (Davis and Sumara 1997). Thus, a classroom within a dysfunctional school can be highly effective, which was true in the classrooms of the teachers I studied (Ladson-Billings 1994). This is not to suggest that we should discourage systemic change, but rather that the lack of a schoolwide reform should not preclude individual teachers from developing effective practice within the system. Third, complex systems are qualitatively different from mechanical systems such as cars and computers, which are "merely complicated" (Davis and Sumara, p. 118). One can understand a complicated system by analyzing each of its component parts. This analysis can make the system rule-governed and predictable. Contrast that with the classroom. Merely examining each individual student within the classroom tells the teacher little about the dynamic of the classroom (system). Yet, that is often precisely the approach we take. It is important to know and understand the individuals in the classroom, but it is equally important to understand how the group functions and how individuals relate to, and function within, the group.

Perhaps by melding notions of situated cognition with complexity theory we can provide teachers and researchers with a different type of lens through which to understand the classroom and improve it. If we understand that the multiple contexts in which students live their lives affect the classroom system in a variety of ways, we might begin to create the kinds of mathematics curricula and pedagogy that take full advantage of the adaptive, resilient, complex nature of learners in a classroom. Rather than presuming that because of their race, culture, ethnicity, language, or other form of difference students are unable to succeed in mathematics, this lens might force us to ask how the mathematics we are teaching (and how we teach it) is changing the system. How might we construct mathematics learning situations that improve the system? When we look at other aspects of the curricula where students may be experiencing success, what does that tell us about certain aspects of learning that work well in a classroom system?

Certainly there is enough literature documenting the mathematics failure of African American students. Where a lack occurs is in the documentation of successful practice of mathematics for African American students. The challenge of improving the mathematical performance of African American students must be fought on three fronts—programmatic, personal, and political. Programmatically, we must participate in the development of meaningful and challenging curricula. Personally, we must come to develop caring and compassionate relationships with students—relationships born out of informed empathy, not sympathy. And, politically, we must understand that our future as a people is directly tied to our children's ability to make the most of their education—to use it not merely for their own economic gain and personal aggrandizement, but rather for a restructuring of an inequitable, unjust society. Our students have immeasurable talents and innumerable strengths. That they do not do well in school in general, and in mathematics in particular, just doesn't add up.

References

Ayers, William. "The Shifting Ground of Curriculum Thought and Everyday Practice." *Theory into Practice* 31 (1992): 259-63.

Boykin, A. Wade, and Forist Toms. "Black Child Socialization: A Conceptual Framework." In *Black Children: Social, Educational, and Parental Environments*, edited by Harriet McAdoo and James McAdoo. Beverly Hills, Calif.: Sage, 1985.

Carnegie Corporation of New York. "Renegotiating Society's Contract with the Public Schools." *Carnegie Quarterly* 29/30 (1984/85): 1-4, 6-11.

Carpenter, Thomas, and Elizabeth Fennema. "Research and Cognitively Guided Instruction." In *Integrating Research on Teaching and Learning Mathematics*, edited by Elizabeth Fennema, Thomas P. Carpenter, and Susan J. Lamon, pp. 2-19. Madison: University of Wisconsin, National Center for Research in Mathematical Sciences Education, 1988.

Casti, John L. *Complexification: Explaining a Paradoxical World through the Science of Surprise.* New York: HarperCollins, 1994.

Clark, Septima, and Cynthia Brown, eds. *Ready from Within: A First Person Narrative.* Trenton, N.J.: Africa World Press, 1990.

Cole, Michael, John Gay, Joseph A. Glick, and Donald W. Sharp. *The Cultural Context of Learning and Thinking: An Exploration in Experimental Anthropology.* New York: Basic Books, 1971.

Davis, Brent, and David D. Sumara. "Cognition, Complexity, and Teacher Education." *Harvard Educational Review* 67 (1997): 105-25.

Fasheh, Munir. "Community Education: To Reclaim and Transform What Has Been Made Invisible." *Harvard Educational Review*, 60 (1990): 19-35.

Fennema, Elizabeth, Megan Franke, Thomas Carpenter, and Deborah Carey. "Using Children's Mathematical Knowledge in Instruction." *American Educational Research Journal* 30 (1993): 555-84.

Foster, Michele. "Sociolinguistics and the African American Community: Implications for Literacy." *Theory into Practice* 31 (1992): 303-11.

Freire, Paulo. *Pedagogy of the Oppressed.* New York: Continuum, 1970.

Grant, S. G., Penelope Peterson, and Angela Shojgreen-Downer, "Learning to Teach Mathematics in the Context of Systemic Reform." *American Educational Research Journal* 33 (1996): 509-41.

Haberman, Martin. "The Pedagogy of Poverty Versus Good Teaching." *Phi Delta Kappan* 73 (1991): 290-94.

Jetter, A. "Mississippi Learning." *New York Times Magazine* 21 (February 1993): 30-35, 50-51, 64, 72.

Ladson-Billings, Gloria. *The Dreamkeepers: Successful Teachers for African American Children.* San Francisco: Jossey-Bass, 1994.

———. "Toward a Theory of Culturally Relevant Teaching." *American Educational Research Journal* 33 (1995): 465-91.

Miller, Jerome G. "African American Males in the Criminal Justice System." Kappan Special Report. *Phi Delta Kappan* 78 (June 1997): K1-K12.

Morris, Aldon. *The Origins of the Civil Rights Movement*. New York: Free Press, 1984.

Oakes, Jeannie, Tor Ormseth, Robert Bell, and Patricia Camp. *Multiplying Inequalities: The Effects of Race, Social Class, and Tracking on Opportunities to Learn Mathematics and Science*. Santa Monica, Calif: Rand Corporation, 1990.

Orr, Ellanor. *Twice as Less*. Markham, Ont.: Penguin Books, 1987.

Putnam, Ralph, Magdalene Lampert, and Penelope Peterson. "Alternative Perspectives on Knowing Mathematics in Elementary Schools." In *Review of Research in Education*, vol. 16, edited by C. Cazden, pp. 57–150. Washington, D.C.: American Educational Research Association, 1990.

Secada, Walter G. "Race, Ethnicity, Social Class, Language, and Achievement in Mathematics." In *Handbook of Research on Mathematics Teaching and Learning,* edited by Douglas A. Grouws, pp. 623-60. New York: Macmillan, 1992.

Shulman, Lee. "Knowledge and Teaching: Foundations of the New Reform." *Harvard Educational Review* 57 (1987): 1–22.

Smith, Laura Brooks and Lee V. Stiff. "Restructuring the Teaching of High School General Mathematics and Pre-Algebra to the Least Academically Prepared Students." Paper presented at the annual meeting of the American Educational Research Association, Atlanta, Ga., April 1993.

Stein, Mary Kay, Barbara W. Grover, and Marjorie Henningsen. "Building Student Capacity for Mathematical Thinking and Reasoning: An Analysis of Mathematical Tasks Used in Reform Classrooms." *American Educational Research Journal* 33 (1996): 455–88.

Stevenson, Harold. *The Learning Gap*. New York: Summit Books, 1992.

Tate, William F. "Race, Retrenchment, and the Reform of School Mathematics." *Phi Delta Kappan* 75 (1994): 477-85.

United States Department of Education. (1996). *Pursuing Excellence: Initial Findings from the Third International Mathematics and Science Study*. Washington, D.C.: Office of Educational Research and Improvement, 1996.

Waldrop, M. Mitchell. *Complexity: The Emerging Science at the Edge of Order and Chaos*. New York: Simon & Schuster, 1992.

Whitaker, Charles. "A Generation in Peril." *Ebony* (August 1988): 34-36.

The Politics of Urban Mathematics Education

Stephen R. Cox
Temple University

What are the politics of urban mathematics education? Local, state, and national education communities are acknowledging the fact that American students, particularly minority urban students, are not performing mathematically at levels that will keep the United States in pace with its foreign counterparts. The current state of education dictates that we, as a nation, must create a more effective system to ensure a quality education for all our students.

In most of our urban centers, we are responsible for educating large numbers of students who have the same educational needs as other American students. In some circumstances, however, urban students are hampered by inadequate facilities, overcrowded classrooms, minimal access to technology, and teachers who lack confidence in their students' abilities to achieve significant levels of understanding in core and advanced mathematics curricula.

Questions of Full Participation in Mathematics

One could argue that the substantial baggage that urban students bring to their educational situations hampers their ability to learn and increases their potential for academic failure. This argument negates the effectiveness of schools; it allows for no mediation on the part of the school, the principal, or the teacher to meet the challenges and improve the learning environment. Could there be some alternative strategy for improving the educational environment that the education community has overlooked? Can we offer solutions to urban educational challenges? What about the national movement for education reform? What is the mechanism for education reform? How do we move our schools from their present dysfunctional state to a functional and productive condition?

Finding a Solution

The African proverb "It takes a whole village to raise a child" is a much used phrase but is only partially understood by the broader community. At this time, the proverb could be "It takes a whole village to save a child." How does one engage the community or village in becoming vested in this initiative of both raising and saving our youth? The truth reveals that at the most fundamental level, each one of us is responsible for creating an environment that ensures success in education for all our children. Colleges and universities, school districts, administrators, teachers, parents, industries, and community organizations must consider themselves at war with the forces that inhibit urban students' success in education.

During the last ten years, I have been involved in a sequence of major national initiatives to improve mathematics and science literacy in the continental United States and Puerto Rico. Funded primarily by the National Science Foundation, the Department of Education, other governmental agencies, and a host of private foundations and corporations, these initiatives have focused on the education of underrepresented students from kindergarten through graduate school. At the heart of these initiatives was the politics of bringing together the stakeholders in the community. Organizing a group of diverse players into a functional team is complex. It requires patience, access to effective research, strategic planning, and some good fortune. You may notice that funding was not mentioned; this is not an oversight on my part. Funding plays a role only when the reform team is organized and correctly constituted.

Where Are We Now?

Let me first address the state of urban mathematics education. In the last twenty years, national statistics have evidenced the lack of performance of African American, Latino, and Native American students in science, engineering, and mathematics in both precollege and undergraduate programs. Two major impediments that contribute to the poor performance of these students are (1) the lack of opportunity to participate in higher-level courses and (2) screening mechanisms such as the Scholastic Assessment Test (SAT). These impediments are interwoven. In many of our urban high schools, students are not challenged to pursue or encouraged to enter mathematics and scientific career fields. If students are not prepared for, and enrolled in, advanced mathematics courses so that they can reach a level of proficiency, then the probability of their entering and being successful in most undergraduate programs, regardless of the disciplinary focus, is nil. Many colleges use the SAT as a filter when deciding which students, including ethnic minorities, to admit into undergraduate programs. Preparation for the SAT is conducted in our nation's high schools. If African American students are not challenged or encouraged in academic mathematics and science classes, then it is not likely that they will achieve any measure of success on the SAT.

Now, if an informed and well-educated public can influence political decisions about education and the ensuing funding, then we might suggest that urban students have been targeted for exclusion from a solid, useful, meaningful education. If we were to look at the statistics of the last twenty years and assess the collective productivity of urban schools and their contribution to the mathematics and scientific workforce, we would find that the statistics are alarming but not surprising. The number of minority students entering undergraduate science, engineering, mathematics, and technology (SEMT) curricula and the students' subsequent lack of success tell a tale of insensitivity, inadequate preparation, and lack of informed counseling, the sum of which is a formula for decreasing the probability of success for our students.

The decrease in the number of baccalaureate degrees earned by underrepresented students in science, engineering, and mathematics has become a national issue for the United States and is reflected in the trends shown by the Bureau of Labor Statistics. The data substantiate quite dramatically that we have a great deal of work ahead of us if we are to turn the tide and increase our students' successes at the precollege and college levels. The current assessment of our national needs for a scientific and technological workforce indicates that approximately 600 000 scientists, engineers, and mathematicians will be needed if the United States is to be competitive with its foreign counterparts in the next century. I believe that the most important population to target to fill these needs is the population that is currently underrepresented in SEMT.

Policy as a Tool to Improve Participation

Let me tell you what I consider to be one useful mechanism to improve the potential and probability of students' success in the SEMT and, more specifically, in mathematics. The first step is to build a consortium of committed participants and stakeholders dedicated to improving education. On a local level we have had some measure of success building such a consortium in Philadelphia. The success we have experienced in programs funded by the National Science Foundation's Initiatives in the Delaware Valley has been enhanced and improved by the partnerships and collaborations that have continued beyond the funding cycle (see fig. 1). For example, relationships among colleges and universities, school districts, minority professional organizations, community groups and museums, corporate partners, and educational support organizations have proved to be beneficial. Initiatives like the Comprehensive Regional Centers for Minorities (CRCM), the Urban Systemic Initiatives, and the Alliance for Minority Participation developed relationships that have lasted beyond the life of the grants. These collaborative groups are continuing the struggle for educational parity. Each of these initiatives is dedicated to increasing the number of African American, Latino, and Native American students who are interested in and participate in science, engineering, mathematics, and technology careers.

Bringing the appropriate parties together and engaging them in a fundamental strategy to provide an opportunity for all students in SEMT was the primary objective at the outset of the initiatives. What became evident immediately was that committed partners, given multiple strategies, could develop a strong framework for the successful development and implementation of the initiatives. The framework for success was developed using the K–16 pipeline concept as a background for the strategy. Student enrichment programs in grades K–12, undergraduate student programs, improved precollege organizational strategies, and the organization of staff development programs in SEMT, allowed collaborators to participate successfully in this education-reform enterprise. In an environment where education reform and standards development were being organized to meet the needs of the region, these partnerships were in place and facilitated the process of improving our "bottom line"—quality education.

The Philadelphia Algebra Project

The Philadelphia Algebra Project was a collaborative effort of the Philadelphia CRCM and the school district of Philadelphia to increase the number of minority students successfully passing through the district's curricular gateway to higher education and careers in science, mathematics,

Colleges and Universities

- Camden County College
- Cheyney University
- Community College of Philadelphia
- Delaware State University
- Drexel University
- Franklin and Marshall College
- Glassboro State College
- LaSalle University
- Lincoln University
- Montgomery County Community College
- Pennsylvania State University
- Philadelphia College of Pharmacy and Science
- Philadelphia College of Textiles and Science
- Rutgers-Camden University
- St. Joseph's University
- Temple University
- University of Pennsylvania
- University of Pittsburgh
- Villanova University

Minority Professional Organizations

- National Organization for the Advancement of Black Chemists and Chemical Engineering (NOBCChE)
- National Society of Black Engineers (NSBE)
- Society of Hispanic Professionals in Engineering (SHIP)
- National Tech Association (NTA)
- Korean Businessmen's Association
- Hispanic Businessmen's Association

School Districts

- Archdiocese of Philadelphia
- Camden County School District
- Delaware County Public Schools
- School District of Philadelphia
- William Penn School District

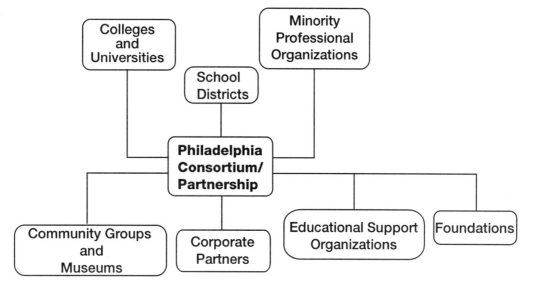

Community Groups and Museums

- ASPIRA
- Executive Service Corporation of the Greater Delaware Valley
- The Franklin Institute
- Omega Psi Phi
- AAAS Black Church PjT

Corporate Partners

- Johnson & Johnson
- Merck Sharpe & Dohme
- Rohm & Haas Company
- ARCO Chemical Company
- Smith Kleine Beecham
- Martin Marietta
- AT & T Bell Labs
- PECO Energy
- Sun Company

Educational Support Organizations

- PRIME
- INROADS
- NACME
- PATHS/PRISM
- CRCM National Centers
- AMP National Alliances

Foundations

- National Science Foundation
- Pew Charitable Trusts
- William Penn Foundation
- Ford Foundation
- Merck Foundation
- Rockefeller Foundation

Fig. 1. Philadelphia Education Fund Alliance partnerships

and engineering. The objectives were the following:

- To strengthen the curriculum and instruction in prealgebra at the seventh and eighth grades
- To introduce more students to algebra at the eighth-grade level in selected schools
- To increase the number of students passing the ninth-grade algebra program
- To encourage more students to take higher-level mathematics and science in high school

Sixty-four schools participated in the project during a two-year period, fifty-three from the School District of Philadelphia and the Philadelphia Archdiocese. Other school districts included Chester Upland and William Penn in Pennsylvania and Camden in New Jersey. In Philadelphia, because of the enthusiasm of the teachers involved in the project, the superintendent of the School District of Philadelphia mandated that all middle schools would offer algebra as a required course.

During year 1 (1989–90), 100 seventh- and eighth-grade middle school mathematics teachers successfully completed intensive professional development courses using the University of Chicago School Mathematics Project materials, which incorporated the National Council of Teachers of Mathematics Standards. These graduate courses covered transition mathematics for seventy-five middle grades teachers of mathematics and twenty-five certified teachers of algebra. The Philadelphia CRCM provided each teacher with a classroom set of scientific calculators, and the algebra teachers received a personal-computer monitor, software, and a computer cart provided by the school district. To reinforce the training, participating teachers had access to a users group that had been established. This group met monthly so that teachers could share and resolve their problems and report their progress in teaching the new material.

The Philadelphia Algebra Project has become one of the most effective programs in the CRCM's arsenal of activities. In the summer following the first sequence of the professional development program, the teachers taught students who would be participating in the following academic year's mathematics program. At the end of the four-week teaching sequence, the teachers reported that they were comfortable with the curriculum and thought that the students would benefit from the experience. Recent assessments of this program show that students who took algebra in the eighth grade had an 85 percent success rate in the first year. This program has had a systemic impact in the School District of Philadelphia and will increase the number of students moving on to higher levels of mathematics and science.

In the year preceding the development of the CRCM, there were 146 students taking algebra in the eighth grade in Philadelphia. In year 4, the number of students enrolled had increased to approximately 2700 students in eighth grade and another 520 students in seventh grade. Of the first students to participate in the project, 95 percent have gone on to take higher-level mathematics and science.

The algebra project has spread down to the fifth and sixth grades through the organizing consortium's development of the pretransition curriculum to support early intervention in the feeder elementary schools. A second growth component has allowed the high schools in the upper end of the feeder pattern to take advantage of the Interactive Mathematics Project, which uses thematic problems in a practical-applications format that will affect the curriculum from algebra through calculus for high school students and teachers.

The Consortium

The lessons learned in this relationship set the tone for the extraordinary policies and initiatives of the Philadelphia school district, for the regional consortium, and for the role of the NSF's Comprehensive Regional Center for Minorities in Philadelphia. The algebra project became the core of the entire CRCM effort; it allowed the professional development of the teachers to transcend mathematics and cross disciplines to include science, African American contributions, and a focus on real-world problem solving.

Although we had discussed the organization of a consortium, the test of this alliance was entering the school district and establishing a relationship to facilitate the staff development of middle school teachers. Issues such as extracurricular time and payment, the cost of graduate credits, the instructors, the curriculum, the selection of the teachers, and the selection of the schools to be involved had to be negotiated with all the appropriate parties. Once these matters were settled, we resolved to meet what all had agreed was the common goal: the improvement of mathematics education.

The establishment and success of this project are evidence that policy decisions by members of a consortium can bring about changes in the education of urban students in mathematics. School systems have to be willing to set policies that encourage the enthusiastic participation of all students, improve the effectiveness and the content knowledge of teachers, and enable the community to be involved in the education of its students.

Professional Development: Finding New Ways to Support Teachers of Minority Students

Marieta W. Harris
Urban Systemic Initiative
Memphis City Schools

If a doctor, lawyer, or dentist had 40 people in his office at one time, all of whom had different needs, and some of whom didn't want to be there and were causing trouble, and the doctor, lawyer, or dentist, without assistance, had to treat them all with professional excellence for nine months, then he might have some conception of the classroom teacher's job.

—Donald O. Quinn

Teachers do not see themselves as true professionals who need ongoing professional development as doctors, lawyers, or dentists do. Professional development for teachers is one of the hottest issues in education. Almost every school district in America has established teacher education and professional development as a strong component of educational reform. Certainly, federal dollars have supported professional development through Title I, Eisenhower, Title VI, and Carl Perkins funds.

Since the publication of *A Nation at Risk* in 1983, the ongoing education of teachers has become the focus of lasting school reform. Professional development, as a prevalent theme in the genuine efforts to reform schools, is highlighted in the recent report of the National Commission on Teaching and America's Future (1996) called *What Matters Most: Teaching for America's Future*. This commission consists of a blue-ribbon panel of educators, policy-makers, and business leaders from around the country who have drawn needed attention to professional development.

Two organizations currently developing exemplary programs for the professional development of teachers are the National Board for Professional Teaching Standards and the National Science Foundation. Both organizations are providing today's educators guidance and support in the development and implementation of professional development programs that are the foundations of systemic reform.

National Board for Professional Teaching Standards

The National Board for Professional Teaching Standards identifies and recognizes teachers who effectively enhance students' learning and demonstrate a high level of knowledge, skills, dispositions, and commitment through five core propositions. These core propositions are included here because, in addition to reflecting standards for teachers, they are especially important to those teachers who are responsible for the mathematics education of African American children.

1. Teachers Are Committed to Students and Their Learning

Teachers should be dedicated to making knowledge accessible to all students. They should act on the belief that all students can learn. They should treat students equitably, recognizing the individual differences that distinguish their students one from the other. They should appropriately adjust their practices according to their observation and knowledge of their students' interests, abilities, skills, knowledge, family circumstances, and peer relationships.

Accomplished teachers understand how students develop and learn, and they are mindful of the influence of context

19

and culture on behavior. They develop students' cognitive capacity and their respect for learning. These teachers foster students' self-esteem, motivation, character, civic responsibility, and respect for individual, cultural, religious, and racial differences.

2. Teachers Know the Subjects They Teach and How to Teach Those Subjects to Students

Teachers of mathematics should have a rich understanding of mathematics and appreciate how this knowledge is created, organized, linked to other disciplines, and applied to real-world settings. Accomplished teachers should have a command of how to convey and reveal subject matter (mathematics) to students. They should know where difficulties are likely to arise and modify their practices accordingly. They should be adept at teaching students how to pose and solve their own problems, and they should bring to the instructional process strategies and instructional materials that can assist students.

3. Teachers Are Responsible for Managing and Monitoring Students' Learning

Teachers must create, enrich, maintain, and alter instructional settings to capture and sustain the interest of their students and to make effective use of time. Accomplished teachers must be skilled at engaging students and adults to assist the teaching being conducted and enlisting their colleagues' knowledge and expertise to complement their own. These teachers know how to work with groups of students to ensure a disciplined learning environment. They set norms for social interaction among students and motivate students to learn to maintain interest even in the face of temporary failure. Teachers who monitor their students' learning use multiple sources of evidence of students' growth and understanding and can clearly communicate students' performance to both the students and their parents.

4. Teachers Think Systematically about Their Practice and Learn from Experience

Teachers should be models of educated persons who seek to inspire students by exemplifying curiosity, tolerance, honesty, fairness, respect for diversity, and appreciation of cultural differences. NBPTS Board–certified teachers, including those who are charged to teach mathematics to African American students, should continually examine their practice, seeking to expand their repertoire, deepen their knowledge, sharpen their judgment, and adapt their teaching to new findings, ideas, and theories.

5. Teachers Are Members of Learning Communities

Exemplary teachers should contribute to the effectiveness of the school by working collaboratively with other professionals on instructional policy, curriculum development, and staff development. They should evaluate their school's progress and the allocation of school resources in light of their understanding of state and local standards. They should be knowledgeable about specialized school and community resources that can be engaged for their students' benefit, and they should be skilled at employing such resources as needed. They should work creatively with parents, engaging them productively in the work of the school.

These five core propositions of the National Board for Professional Teaching Standards serve as a foundation for the creation of appropriate professional development initiatives for teachers. Professional development has drawn much attention in the past two years. Mathematics educators are seeking to gain a better understanding of the role that professional development plays in sustaining systemic, standards-based school reform and improving student achievement in mathematics. The issues around professional development are enhanced as we consider professional development programs for teachers who serve in urban districts.

The National Science Foundation's Systemic Initiatives

Each of the systemic initiatives funded by the National Science Foundation (NSF) is required to—

- significantly improve learning leading to high achievement in challenging science and mathematics by all students;
- establish a system that supports such improved learning so that it sustains this accomplishment over time.

Professional development is one of eight fundamental elements that must be addressed by each systemic initiative: instruction; standards; curriculum; assessment; professional development; policy; leadership, governance, and management; and partnership and public awareness. In addition, the cross-cutting variables that play an integrating role in the operation of the initiative are equity, quality, scaling-up, and coordination and organization.

NSF (1997) has provided six "drivers" for educational system reform that specify expected changes in the system. Drivers 1 and 2 both directly address professional development and are identified in figure 1. Response to Driver 1 requires that those responsible consider answers to two fundamental questions. First, we must consider the extent to which there is an ongoing professional development program in place that provides teachers and other staff with the skills and knowledge to implement high-quality mathematics and science curricula. This consideration is fundamental because for too long, high-quality mathematics and science curricula have not been made available to African American students. Second, we must ask the question, Do all teachers, teacher aides, and other staff participate in the professional develop-

Driver 1

Implementation of comprehensive, standards-based curricula as represented in instructional practice, including student assessment, in every classroom, laboratory, and other learning experience provided through the system and its partners.

Fundamental Questions on Professional Development

1.5: To what extent is there an ongoing professional development program in place that provides teachers and other staff with the skills and knowledge to implement the high-quality curriculum?

1.6: To what extent do all teachers, teachers' aides, and other staff participate in the professional development program?

Driver 2

Development of a coherent, consistent set of policies that support provisions of high-quality mathematics and science education for each student; excellent preparation, continuing education, and support for each mathematics and science teacher (including all elementary school teachers); and other learning experiences provided through the system and its partners.

Fundamental Questions on Professional Development

2.4: To what extent do policies support the preservice education of a high-quality teaching force in mathematics and science?

2.5: To what extent do policies assure adequate time for the ongoing professional development of mathematics and science teachers?

2.7: To what extent do policies assure adequate financial and administrative support for the ongoing development of mathematics and science teachers?

2.8: To what extent are policies designed to recognize and reward excellence in mathematics and science teaching?

Fig. 1. National Science Foundation systemic reform questions on professional development

ment program? This question is important in urban districts because the large size of the student and teacher populations and limited funding and staff does not allow many teachers of African American students to participate in high-quality professional development programs.

As one considers professional development in its relationship to policy changes needed for reform in mathematics and science education, fundamental issues arise. Driver 2 provides a frame for this consideration. First, do policies support the preservice education of a high-quality teaching force in mathematics and science? The future success of urban districts will depend on the availability of an adequate pool of highly qualified mathematics and science teachers from which to draw. That pool of qualified African American teachers is almost nonexistent.

Second, we must consider whether existing policies assure adequate financial and administrative support for the ongoing professional development of mathematics and science teachers. Urban districts must indicate that professional development for teachers is valued and demonstrate their concern by furnishing administrative and financial support for high-quality professional development initiatives.

Third, policies must recognize and reward excellence in mathematics and science teaching. For too long, teachers in urban districts have had to recognize and reward themselves for high levels of commitment and quality teaching. They have had to depend on intrinsic rewards related to seeing their students succeed.

The professional development of teachers is central to any genuine efforts to reform school districts and schools. Continuous teacher training and development are essential to the achievement of standards-driven outcomes. Researchers indicate that the nation's reform agenda requires that most teachers must reinvent their teaching practices and set higher standards for themselves and for their students. Such changes will allow us to establish a rationale for professional development programs.

Rationale

Rankin (1996) uses the work of Darling-Hammond and McLaughlin as he indicates that "the vision of practice underlying the nation's reform agenda requires most teachers to reconceptualize their practice, to construct new classroom roles and expectations about student outcomes, and to teach in ways they have never taught before and probably have never experienced" (p. 2). Rankin further adds that "the success of the agenda turns ultimately on teachers' success in accomplishing the serious and difficult tasks of learning skills and perspectives assumed by new visions of practice and, often, unlearning practices and beliefs about students or instruction that have dominated their entire professional lives" (p. 2).

Kaufman (1997) discusses the improvement of educational outcomes for all students as it relates to professional development. He says that we must promote a professional development process for teachers that interweaves curricular and instructional reform and equity reform. We generally attack the problem of inequity by reallocating tangible resources, by assuring that schools and teachers change mathematics content through professional development, and by providing resources to support reform in assessment methods. However, little has been done to help educators change institutional bias or individual teaching practices that are inequitable.

Kaufman (1997) proposes four basic elements—stance, decision making, best practices, and teacher leadership—for a system of professional development that will assure equal access to students, provide equal resources, and produce equitable outcomes. I will use these elements as a basis for a professional development program that can help teachers of African American students be more successful.

Stance

Traditionally, professional development (in-service training) has assumed a stance toward practice that concentrates on conveying information, providing ideas, and training in skills that are generally related to content and pedagogy. This information presents teachers with an enormous assortment of resources, but the teacher's potential is restricted by the lack of critical discussion about how these resources can be used in instruction. It is certain that teachers must engage in practice that includes critical inquiry, examination, trial, and debate. They must examine research critically and change their practice and programs accordingly.

Decision Making

In order for educators to know that we are removing barriers to educational opportunities for all students, we must be prepared to ask probing questions about student achievement, classroom practice, and district policies. This means that we must collect and analyze data in each area. Traditionally, teachers have not been engaged in this kind of work. The collection and interpretation of data has been left to the district office, the state department of education, or university researchers. The results of data analysis have been handed to teachers along with prescriptions for "fixing" the problems. Little information has been gathered at the level of classroom practice, and teachers have not been assisted in becoming reflective about their practice. As a result, teachers own neither the problem nor the solution. In order to remedy this situation, professional development must include a stance of critique and inquiry that allows teachers to gather, analyze, and use data about their classrooms and their students.

Best Practices

Professional development must make available to teachers a growing body of knowledge about effective instruction and high-quality curricula. As teachers become learners of mathematics and are introduced to powerful ideas and ways to teach them, they invariably find ways to translate that learning back into their classrooms. It is important that educators subject curriculum materials to rigorous standards in order to assure that time is not spent with less effective approaches and materials that will delay the process of reform and the ultimate impact on student achievement.

Teacher Leadership

True professional development results in the creation of teacher-leaders. Teachers can become advocates for reform when they are engaged in inquiry, critical analysis, and problem solving and have access to high-quality curricula. Teachers must have experiences that allow them to gain new knowledge, habits of mind, and individual and social resources that will allow the reform to prosper. In Memphis, teachers who are involved in providing instruction and leadership in district-level safety-net activities for students are able to shape their own instructional practices. The experiences that they have in creating unique learning experiences for students in Saturday Academy, Algebra Camp, and the Algebra Extended-Year Program can be translated into their regular classrooms and shared with colleagues.

Two related professional development issues must be examined as we consider mathematics education reform in African American communities. Preservice preparation and teacher certification are significant because the preparation of teachers prior to entering the profession has a direct effect on the kind and quantity of professional development that is required once they are actual practitioners.

Preservice Preparation

Preservice programs must rely on teachers teaching teachers. This idea stems from the belief that if one wants to know how to teach well, one must seek out the wise counsel of an able colleague. Colleges of education must consult with the practitioners within schools for counsel about content, pedagogy, assessment, and effective use of technology as a tool for instruction. This kind of collaboration cannot be limited to one-semester assignments in courses that have been traditionally labeled as "student teaching."

Additionally, along these lines, the Memphis Urban Systemic Initiative (USI) has established a collaborative link with the Memphis Alliance for Minority Participation Program. Memphis USI employs student mentors for its student support activities such as Saturday Academy, Algebra Camp, and the Algebra Extended-Year Program. Student mentors include college and university students who are studying mathematics, science, technology, and teacher education. Their experiences as student mentors allow them the opportunity to interact with middle school and high school students and to observe and participate in educational reform practices.

Teacher Certification

Increasing the number of certified teachers is essential to achieve the goals of systemic reform in mathematics, science, and technology education. The statistics related to teacher certification indicate that there is an extreme deficit in qualified and certified mathematics and science teachers. The shortfall of qualified minority teachers is even more extreme. This is a national phenomenon and should be addressed by all districts that are engaged in mathematics and science education reform. Teachers must be supported by the district and by colleges and universities in gaining state certification. District leaders must develop and implement mentor programs that support new and nontenured teachers. Similarly, they must recruit from among those high school students who have the potential to become mathematics and science teachers.

The policies that schools use to assign teachers to classrooms and courses are primary determinants of how teachers develop a sense of a shared community within individual schools. Policies that isolate or create elite groups of teachers do little to foster the collegial relationships and a shared sense of purpose that teachers need in order to reflect on their work.

Additionally, there are basic requisites for teachers of minority students. These requisites should be included in professional development programs for teachers who are specifically charged with the mathematics education of African American students. Teachers should (*a*) be prepared to teach educationally unprepared students, (*b*) develop a second language skill, (*c*) develop "street smarts," (*d*) be aware of students' cultural and ethnic history, (*e*) examine and understand intercultural differences, and (*f*) find a mentor.

Conclusion

School districts are beginning to see the virtue in investing time and effort in the establishment of a quality teaching force. Teachers must be trained prior to entering the profession, but they must also be given the opportunity to keep current in their subject matter and to learn new skills and new ways to involve their students in the learning process. The National Board for Professional Teaching Standards and the National Science Foundation's drivers for systemic reform provide the foundation for developing and implementing professional development for all teachers. Education reform as espoused by districts across the country present a rationale for changes in the quality and extent of professional development. Professional development must be consistent with the standards-based outcomes that are expected and that result in quality instruction programs and classroom practice. Professional development must also address the specific requisites for those who are responsible for teaching African American students.

Professional development in this era of mathematics reform should support site-based teachers, schools involved in renewal activities, innovative programs, and learning. Districts and schools must strive to coordinate and integrate staff development into the everyday practice of teachers. Learning must permeate everything that the district and the school do. All of us who are held responsible must ensure that professional development is designed to create individual and organizational habits and structures that make continuous learning a valued and endemic part of the culture of schools and teaching. Teachers must be provided the opportunity to "stretch" their understanding and skills.

References

Kaufman, Mark. "A Professional Development Stance for Equity." *SSI Perspective News about Systemic Reform* 2, no. 3: 4–5.

Hill, Howard. *Effective Strategies for Teaching Minority Students.* Bloomington, Ind.: National Educational Service, 1989.

National Commission on Excellence in Education. *A Nation at Risk.* Washington, D.C.: U.S. Government Printing Office, 1983.

National Commission on Teaching and America's Future. *What Matters Most: Teaching for America's Future.* New York: Teachers College, Columbia University, 1996.

National Science Foundation, Directorate of Education and Human Resources, Division of Educational System Reform. *Administrative Manual for Systemic Initiative Awardees.* Washington, D.C.: National Science Foundation, 1997.

National Science Foundation. *Indicators of Science and Mathematics Education.* Washington, D.C.: National Science Foundation, 1995.

Rankin, John. "Transforming Professional Development." *NSF Systemic Initiatives Newsletter* 1 (October 1996): 1–2.

The National Science Foundation's Innovative Curriculum Materials Program

Glenda Lappan
Michigan State University

I am pleased to discuss the NSF projects that were funded to create grades K–12 curriculum materials consistent with the NCTM *Curriculum and Evaluation Standards for School Mathematics* (1989) and *Professional Standards for Teaching Mathematics* (1991). I have an enormous responsibility. It is one thing to represent yourself and your own work; it is quite another to try to represent a whole collection of projects. I am going to restrict my discussion to the set of complete curricula that have been funded and developed in the past six years and do my best to help you understand the fundamental driving forces behind this effort.

There are three projects funded at the elementary school level, five at the middle school level, and four at the secondary level. Figure 1 includes the names of the projects and the project directors, as well as the publishers and telephone contact numbers, if available. As you can see from the figure, this is quite an impressive array of work. The very names of the projects suggest that something new is afoot—Maths in Context, Connected Mathematics Project, Core-Plus Mathematics, and such.

Overall Project Goals

When we wrote the *Curriculum and Evaluation Standards* and the *Professional Teaching Standards*, one of the stances that we as a community took was that every child has the right to an excellent mathematics education. Inclusion—mathematics for all—was the commitment we pushed ourselves to make as a nation. Each of these NSF projects was challenged to produce a complete curriculum for a span of grades that focused on important mathematics for *all* students. The NCTM *Standards* documents served as guideposts for the curriculum decisions that were made by the projects. Each group of developers made a strong com-

mitment to creating materials that would help a teacher in a classroom make mathematics accessible to every child and to help that teacher believe in the mathematics education of every child. Following is a set of commitments that we've all made to children (Lappan 1997):

- *Inclusiveness.* Effective mathematics teaching and learning should be experienced by every student with the commitment to developing mathematical power for all students.

- *Depth over coverage.* Curriculum, instruction, and assessment should emphasize a smaller number of big, powerful ideas.

- *Understanding.* Curriculum, instruction, and assessment should be aligned to foster genuine understanding of the big ideas and processes in mathematics.

- *Active engagement.* Genuine learning requires active mental and, at times, physical engagement, as well as efforts to understand and use ideas.

- *Investigations.* Deep understanding is best promoted by posing problems and questions and then skillfully guiding problem solving and discourse so that students' ideas are constantly probed and pushed toward more powerful mathematical realizations.

- *Application.* Curriculum, instruction, and assessment should foster an ability and a disposition to use mathematical ideas and processes flexibly to solve nonroutine problems, which come from real-world contexts as well as from mathematics itself.

- *Connections.* Deep understanding involves making connections between one's informal knowledge of mathematics and the more formal mathematics and mathemat-

Elementary Mathematics Curriculum Projects

Everyday Math	Max Bell Everyday Learning 1-312-708-1563
Investigations	Susan Jo Russell, Jim Kaput, Doug Clements, Mike Battista Dale Seymour Publications 1-800-417-2321 1-800-872-1100
Math Trailblazers	Phil Wagreich, Howard Goldberg Kendall Hunt Publishers 1-800-770-3544

Middle School Mathematics Curriculum Projects

Connected Mathematics Project (CMP)	Glenda Lappan, Betty Phillips, Bill Fitzgerald, Jim Fey, Susan Friel Dale Seymour Publications 1-800-417-2321 1-800-872-1100
Mathematics through Applications	Shelly Goldman, Ray McDermott, James Greeno, George Pake c/o Doris Perkins 1-415-614-7900
Maths in Context	Tom Romberg Britannica 1-608-263-4285
Mathscape	Glenn Kleiman, Elizabeth Bjork Creative Publications 1-800-357-MATH
STEM	Rick Billstein, Johnny Lott, Barbara Byrd McDougal Littel/Houghton Mifflin 1-800-289-2558 x3364

High School Mathematics Curriculum Projects

ARISE	Landy Godbold, Solomon Garfunkel COMAP, Inc. 1-800-772-6627
Core-Plus Mathematics Project	Arthur Coxford, Christian Hirsch, James Fey, Hal Schoen Everyday Learning 1-800-322-6284
Interactive Mathematics Project	Lynne Alper, Daniel Fendel, Sherry Frazier, Diane Resek Key Curriculum Press 1-800-995-MATH
The Secondary Mathematics Core Curriculum Initiative	June Ellis 1-800-244-1942

Fig. 1. NSF Instructional Materials Development Program

ical language of the discipline as well as among areas of mathematics and between mathematics and other disciplines.

Once you have made that set of commitments, what, then, is the reform about? We set out to update, upgrade, and reform the curriculum itself for numerous reasons of which we are all aware. However, we also need improved classroom instruction and a totally different approach to figuring out what students know from their classroom interactions with mathematical tasks. This called for the development of different and more powerful assessment tools.

Another set of concerns was that we felt we had to develop mathematics programs for schools that are developmentally responsive. I have been terribly concerned during my professional life about the uses of the phrase *developmentally appropriate*. I have seen it used so many times as an excuse not to give children demanding, exciting, challenging mathematics. Yet, we still have to keep in mind that these programs have to be responsive to students. The programs, the mathematics materials, have to reach out and pull children in, connect with children, make what we are doing interesting to children. Programs have to be academically excellent, and they have to be socially equitable. We have to be able to put in the hands of teachers materials that at least give them a crack at creating the kinds of classroom environments that have been envisioned in all the conversations that we've had so far at this meeting and at many other meetings that are taking place across the country. In the *Curriculum and Evaluation Standards*, we put forward four process goals—problem solving, reasoning, communicating, and connecting—that have become the essence of how we talk about mathematics education. The question that we, as curriculum developers, had to answer was how to write a curriculum that will build the most powerful mathematics education that we can for children as it helps realize these four process goals.

But one cannot talk about curriculum for more than thirty seconds without talking about the interaction of that curriculum with children in the classroom. As I look at the work that we have done over the past seven years, one thing that all of us involved have come to understand is that it is very difficult to write exciting, what I call "wall to wall" curricula—in other words, materials that take on the responsibility for the total mathematics education of a child. Although writing such curriculum material is very challenging, it pales in comparison to the challenge of helping teachers envision, believe in, and carry out in their classrooms a different kind of teaching. Consequently, the teaching aspect of these materials has become for all of us quite a remarkable challenge. Yet, you can change the curriculum, and you can change the teaching; but if you do not change the ways in which you work to come to appreciate and understand what sense children are making of mathematics, you certainly are not going to get anywhere. We all have had to take responsibility in these projects for the related aspects of a good curriculum—content, teaching, and assessment—as a united, integrated, thoughtful package.

The Projects

The development of these NSF materials was stimulated by the work of NCTM. But NCTM for me is us. NCTM is the spokesperson for us as teachers of mathematics. The NCTM *Standards* were in the hands of teachers and mathematics educators, and all of us were collectively saying, "We have to cause a revolution in this country for children." We could not have done this curriculum work if the National Science Foundation had not stepped forward and said, "With the *Standards*, it is time for us to put some money into determining whether or not development teams can build curriculum materials with the kind of support for teachers and the kind of assessments that can actually move us forward." In 1990, as a result of the existence of the *Standards* and the willingness of NSF to act, three elementary school curriculum projects were funded; five middle school projects were funded in 1991; and four high school projects were funded in 1992. Everyone in positions of leadership should become familiar with these materials.

The curriculum materials are in different stages of development and publication. Most of those for the elementary and middle grades, and some of the high school materials, are available for purchase. The Connected Mathematics Project has been working for six years. About two months ago we sent off the last edits of the materials; I did not think we could do it in six years.

I am excited that today we can speak of multiple projects. If any one of us were standing alone through this process, we would have little hope of causing needed change. But the collective weight of this set of projects gives me the greatest hope that we might actually be able to accomplish something in this country. These projects have many things in common (although there are differences in the degree to which some of the common principles are carried in the different projects).

Commonalities

Certainly changes in curriculum are challenging to bring off. However, changes in the supporting pedagogy are even more difficult to accomplish. It has been a major focus of the projects working with trial teachers across the country to create student and teacher materials with an eye to teacher learning. Bruner (1960, p. xv) sums up the philosophy of the projects' authors in *The Process of Education*:

> If it [new curriculum] cannot change, move, perturb, inform teachers, it will have no effect on those they teach. It must first and foremost be a curriculum for teachers. If it has any effect on pupils, it will have it by virtue of having an effect on teachers.

What do we have in common? If you look through these materials, regardless of the grade levels at which you are looking—elementary, middle, or high school—the curriculum materials turn instruction and learning around. The materials start by giving students an opportunity to explore mathematical ideas. When that exploration has taken place, the teacher and students work together to make sense of the mathematics embedded in the problems.

The Role of the Teacher

The teacher helps students to draw out the mathematics and make it explicit. Abstracting ideas from our common set of experiences is very important. It's one of the things that all these projects have worked to try to provide—help for teachers on how one thinks in that way. In all these materials, the kinds of problems we developed have the characteristics described in the *Professional Teaching Standards* and the *Curriculum and Evaluation Standards*—problems in which there is no one correct way to solve or work on the problem—problems that involve multiple strategies and that invite students to think about mathematics in different ways.

The projects are working to raise the level of responsibility that students have for their own learning, both inside and outside of class. Tom Cooney at the University of Georgia talks about the amazement of some visitors from Germany when they looked at schools in the Athens Georgia, area. After looking at U.S. classes over several days, the German visitors indicated that American teachers work so very hard but the children do not seem to be doing much of anything. We are trying to turn that around. Yes, the role of the teacher is an incredibly important one, but the role of the student and his or her responsibility for his or her own sense making becomes equally, if not more, important.

Mathematical Tasks and Kinds of Engagement

What makes these materials collectively alike, and very different from texts of the past, are the tasks through which mathematics is learned by students. Every project has made a commitment to contextualized mathematics. Obviously, these words are interpreted differently by each project. In some of the projects, real-world applications are the focus. The mathematics arises out of engaging with, understanding, modeling, and solving real-world problems. In other projects, data and statistics are the driving force. In yet others, contexts are of varied types, from fantasy to real world to mathematics itself. Students have an opportunity to work on bigger problems in a classroom environment that encourages and supports students' interactions with one another and with the teacher. Some projects consider cooperative groups as the primary organizational structure for students. Other projects have a mix of individual, group, and whole-class work. In these project materials, the problems match

the organization of students. For group work to be effective for students, there has to be enough challenge in the problem to make it obviously more productive to work in groups. The conversation and argumentation that groups have on interesting, big problems pushes the learning of every student.

The materials are trying to stimulate classrooms in which questions of sensibility, such as "Why do you think that is so?" and "Is this reasonable?" are asked. I look at answers that my university students give me on mathematics problems. They are so unreasonable that two seconds of thought would tell you that the answer is not correct. What we are trying to do is create classroom environments in which children are asking themselves these questions: What's going on here? Why do I think it's going on? Is my answer reasonable? Does this fit the situation? These materials, all of them—every single project—are built on the premise that if we give children more interesting, bigger, more challenging problems, then we are going to engage their intellect in ways that far exceed what we have been able to do in the past.

The notion that we are going to give children a challenge is one that frightens some teachers, but it exhilarates others. I have these "real down-home ways" of thinking about things. There are two kinds of bread in this world, one is the kind that my husband used to like. (He has lived with me long enough now for me to have changed this.) He used to like that white bread that sticks to the roof of your mouth when you take a bite. I like the kind of bread that you really have to work to eat—I like bread that fights back. I think what these curriculum projects are trying to do is to engage kids in chewing on some of that twelve-grain bread. When you finish chewing on that, you know you've had "a good eat." That is what we are trying to do with the materials that we are creating. And once you give students these more challenging tasks, you have to know how the tasks are working.

All the projects have assessment components to help teachers find out what sense students are making of the mathematics. The *Assessment Standards* (NCTM 1995) influenced the projects as they developed their assessments. These assessment parts of the projects vary from pairs or groups working on performance tasks together to check-ups that look quite traditional to embedded assessments that give daily opportunities for teachers to observe what students are learning. With new content, new instructional strategies, new technology, and new assessment demands, these materials must be supported by professional development opportunities for teachers.

Challenge to Professional Development

These curricula do not walk down a traditional path; they change the way in which students meet and interact with mathematics. Consequently, one of the immense problems that we face is the challenge of professional development for teachers. The professional development programs that have to support these materials (I would claim, any serious attempt to educate every child in America in mathematics) must provide teachers with not only a deeper knowledge of mathematics but a very much broader view of the curriculum and how it develops over time. I do not believe it is sufficient or ever will be sufficient for us to get where we want to go by teachers simply knowing their own grade level of mathematics.

We work hard in our teacher education programs to teach preservice teachers how to write a lesson plan or how to design a unit of instruction. We are finding through these new curriculum materials and our collective work in supporting teachers to grow professionally that teachers must know their grade level extraordinarily well, but they also have to know what experiences children have had previously and where they are going mathematically. This notion of a broader view of the curriculum is one that we have to take seriously. In our teacher education programs at Michigan State University, students graduate having a very good notion of how to plan a single lesson and how to plan a unit, but they have no real, broad sense of how the mathematics they teach fits into the development of children's growing understanding over several years. I think that's a real problem.

Envisioning Classrooms of Learners

The materials we have developed are not meant to be the absolute, unaltered way in which instruction will be delivered in the classroom. Every teacher has a responsibility to his or her students. What a curriculum gives teachers is the groundwork. It gives teachers the spine that can hold their curriculum together. It gives teachers a set of possibilities, but in our professional development programs we have to take on the challenge of helping teachers get smarter about how to adapt the curriculum. Consider working with a problem context that you know will engage children in school in Iowa, in corn country, but not interest children in New York City. What are you going to do? You are going to change the context! You are going to adapt the problem. You are going to work to take the informal knowledge of your own students and that problem and bring them together. In a sense, in spite of having poured six years of my life, seven days a week, about twelve hours a day, into writing curriculum materials, I do not view what we have written as anything other than a platform on which a professional teacher will build his or her practice.

The classroom that we have envisioned across all twelve of these projects is a class in which teachers pose an interesting problem task and children have the means and the opportunity to explore that problem, sometimes individually, sometimes in pairs, sometimes in larger groups, but always in an environment where they can not only ask for help but also receive help. They can give help. They can ask questions. They can challenge one another. They have tools at their disposal to use in making sense of the problem. These tools include manipulatives that students can use to represent their ideas. They also include calculators, graphing calculators, and computers that allow students to explore realistic problems. The ultimate goal is for the students to make sense of the mathematics. Teachers need to develop skill in listening to and assessing what sense their students are making of the mathematics. The question for us is, How do we help teachers have a problem-solving orientation to their teaching, to listen and learn from what their students are saying?

Theory of Teaching

I do not believe that we will ever be smart enough to create an algorithm for teaching. As teachers, we have a responsibility to that classroom of students in front of us. If you are a middle school teacher and you have five classes in the day, each of those classes has a different dynamic and a different need. You have to approach every class as a teacher with the commitment and the mission to solve teaching problems, to find out what it is going to take to engage and teach that particular class, and to reflect on your own practice with the notion of improvement.

What kind of materials can help us to think in these ways? We know a lot about how children make sense of mathematics from the research that has been done by cognitive scientists and curriculum developers. What we do not yet know a lot about is how to take our knowledge of how children make sense of mathematics and translate that into a teaching practice that is a problem-oriented, reflective kind of teaching practice. That view occurs at a time when we are trying to collectively build a theory of teaching. We already have theories of learning. We have wrestled with theories of learning during our lifetimes, but a theory of learning is not a theory of teaching. We have tried in these curriculum projects to provide very different kinds of instructional materials for teachers. We view them as materials that engage teachers in conversations about possibilities. We have used examples from actual classes to show how lessons might play out in the classroom. We show what other teachers have done and how students have reacted. We make suggestions, but not to specify "how" as much as to probe "why."

I want to be really honest about where we are on building this theory of teaching. We have a lot of wild guesses. I think we have a few conjectures, and we have surprisingly few theorems about teaching. We are participants in a period of time when we are trying to get serious about understanding and studying teaching. Problem solving, reasoning, communication, and connections are process goals from the *Standards*. Developing concepts, understanding uses of mathematics, representing one's ideas mathematically, and learning and developing procedures are all student goals for powerful mathematics programs.

Chris Hirsch often talks about one of the high school projects, Core Plus, and pushes what these projects are all about a little further (see fig. 2). He makes a case that the projects are working to provide access to all students. Hirsch uses what I call the D words from the *Standards* in the Core Plus aspects of teaching and learning. We got the word *disposition* from the *Curriculum and Evaluation Standards* and *discourse* from the *Professional Teaching Standards*. These projects are focused on developing students' dispositions—their beliefs about what mathematics is and what mathematical activity is, their perseverance in tackling problems in mathematics, their confidence in themselves as doers of mathematics, and their enthusiasm for mathematics. I am convinced that if we can make some progress here, we will help more children in this country believe that they have access to—and can do—mathematics.

Access to Real Mathematics

Hirsch argues that the commitment to access for all students is helped by giving attention to how students engage in mathematics. We are advocating that these materials are another way of giving children access through the curriculum content, technology, pedagogical approach, and concepts and beliefs of teachers.

Curriculum Content

In these projects, multiple strands nurture differing strengths and talents; content is developed in meaningful, interesting, and diverse contexts; skills are embedded in more global modeling tasks; and technical language and symbols are introduced as the needs arise. You will not see in this set of twelve projects a course labeled algebra or a course labeled geometry. What these projects are about is pushing forward mathematics as an interconnected set of strands. And every year the children in any of these projects are going to have an opportunity to deal with every one of those strands. I have watched so many classrooms in which children shine when geometry is the focus. Another set of children shine when number is the focus. Another set of children shine when probabilistic reasoning is the focus. Children get new beginnings in integrated curricula; they get opportunities to be the person in the class who can help his or her group make sense of something.

All the projects are dealing with contextualized mathematics. Many of the contexts are real-world contexts, some of them are mathematical contexts, some of them are fantasy contexts. Although the projects differ in the nature and mix of contexts used, all support contextualized mathematics for children. Skills are embedded in more global modeling tasks. Now what does that mean? That means that you do not see in any of these projects a page of thirty problems that look just alike. But if you look carefully at these projects, you will see that there's an enormous amount of practice on skills, but it is embedded in interesting problems. Every problem has some bite, some challenge to it.

I have a story about one of the middle school projects. The students went to take the SAT, returned to the classroom, looked at the teacher, and said, "Now that was really a dumb test." The teacher asked what they meant. The students replied that none of the questions on the test made you think—not one! Now that is very different from the past. These curriculum materials are trying not only to develop skills, but also to develop them in contexts where there is never mindless drill. Technical language and symbols are introduced as the need arises. Less emphasis is on "I'm going to tell you how to write mathematics" and more emphasis is on "You're in a problem context and you need to represent your ideas." Children learn how mathematicians represent their ideas. Symbolism is developed and used as it is needed.

Technology

Graphing calculators give children power. The high school projects all use graphing calculators and other technology; the middle school projects are using graphing calculators, at least by grade 7; and all the elementary projects have calculators as tools for children to use to make sense of mathematics. This use of technology promotes versatile ways of dealing with realistic problems. Putting the power of a computing tool in the hand of a youngster reduces the degree to which manipulation is used as a filter, whether we are talking about arithmetic computation or symbol manipulation. Therefore technology is an access issue.

Aspects of Changing Mathematics Teaching and Learning		
Process Goals	**Content**	**Dispositions**
Problem Solving	**Concepts**	**Beliefs**
Reasoning	**Applications**	**Perseverance**
Communication	**Representational Strategies**	**Confidence**
Connections	**Procedures**	**Enthusiasm**

Fig. 2. Aspects of changing mathematics teaching and learning on which projects focus

CHALLENGES IN THE MATHEMATICS EDUCATION OF AFRICAN AMERICAN CHILDREN

Pedagogical Approach

Lessons promote discourse as a central medium for the teacher and the learner to use to build on the student's informal knowledge. The collaborative exploration lets students learn from one another. Pat Campbell has a wonderful way of looking at this. She says you never tell a child something that you can get that child to tell you. I think that's a marvelous way to think of what we are trying to accomplish. Multiple approaches are both possible and valued. The students and teacher work together to make the mathematics that is common to a set of experiences more explicit.

Concepts and Beliefs of Teachers

Are we going after real mathematics? You bet. In all the projects you will see a number strand, you will see a geometry and measurement strand, you will see a probability and statistics strand. And you will see an algebra strand. Not a course, not a point in time in which you suddenly step from here over the algebra boundary. These curriculum materials have algebra as a goal all the way through. There is a development, a more and more sophisticated development, of algebraic skills throughout the grades.

The bottom line for all of us is that we have to help teachers examine their internal beliefs about what children can actually do in mathematics. We know that children can learn more, can think at more abstract levels, and can persevere longer than our past expectations indicated. These NSF projects can help us expand our expectations of what children can do and when they can do it.

Summary

These projects represent a real challenge to "business as usual." They provide a chance to make substantive changes in the depth of our students' engagement with mathematics. They require a commitment by school districts to provide professional development support for teachers over a period of two to three years. They require work on the part of administrators, school boards, and teachers to help parents understand what is to be gained by such changes in the teaching and learning of mathematics.

As good as these new materials are, we must be aware that they are just that—a bold new effort to perturb the system so that all students will have access to good mathematics. If we take advantage of the opportunity, we will all learn much that can be used to build second-generation materials of this sort that come even closer to realizing our vision of mathematical power for every student.

References

Bruner, Jerome S. *The Process of Education*. Cambridge, Mass.: Harvard University Press, 1960.

Hirsch, Christian. "The Core-Plus Curriculum Materials." Paper read at the Summer Workshop of Teacher Education Redesign Group of the Michigan Statewide Systemic Initiative, Traverse City, Mich., July 1997.

Lappan, Glenda. "The Challenges of Implementation: Supporting Teachers." *American Journal of Education* 106 (November 1997): 207-39.

National Council of Teachers of Mathematics. *Assessment Standards for School Mathematics*. Reston, Va.: National Council of Teachers of Mathematics, 1995.

——. *Curriculum and Evaluation Standards for School Mathematics*. Reston, Va.: National Council of Teachers of Mathematics, 1989.

——. *Professional Standards for Teaching Mathematics*. Reston, Va.: National Council of Teachers of Mathematics, 1991.

Assessment, Evaluation, Mathematics Education Reform, and African American Students: A Framework

Frank E. Davis
Lesley College

The purpose of this conference is to identify issues and generate solutions to the challenges associated with the mathematics teaching and learning of African American children. My expertise lies in the area of program evaluation and assessment, and my recent work has involved evaluating educational programs aimed at influencing African American children in rural and inner-city areas. Here, I focus on the issue of assessment from the perspective of classroom teachers.

I think it is clear that assessment and evaluation have always been part of a teacher's work. However, with current efforts of mathematics educational reform, which include an emphasis on (1) teaching that allows students to construct mathematical ideas, (2) teaching that facilitates mathematical discourse, and (3) at least formally recognizing the need for equity, questions about how to carry out assessments in the classroom have become much more complex. Although much more work is being done on producing innovative ways of assessing students that fit aspects of the reform effort and more information is available to teachers (See Herman, Aschbacher, and Winters [1992]), there appears to be an important "bottom line" (Cooney, Badger, and Wilson 1993, p. 247):

> Unless it is understood that new forms of assessment reflect a different and more fundamental vision of what it means to know mathematics, rich and challenging tasks not only will have little relevance to the curriculum but will not be used. Our research has indicated that however innovative the tasks, teachers will not use them for assessment if (1) these tasks do not reflect their own understanding of mathematics, (2) they do not recognize the value of such tasks in measuring significant mathematical knowledge, and (3) they do not value the outcomes the items purport to measure.... As a consequence, a promising vision evaporates into a mirage.

Getting past this bottom line involves understanding the relationships among classroom goals, assumptions about mathematics, mathematics teaching, and the children we teach. The relationships among all these things should also be considered in conjunction with a process of evaluation and assessment.

I shall describe what I perceive to be important goals in the mathematics education of African American students and, therefore, the goals toward which an assessment and evaluation system should be moving. I believe there are three major categories of goals that describe what children should learn, what learning skills and attitudes children should have, and what is necessary to achieve and sustain mathematics educational reform.

Goals for the Mathematics Education of African American Students

What African American children should learn has recently been discussed through the idea of achieving *mathematics literacy*. I mean by this term the mathematics necessary to have access to the economic mainstream of our society as it is continuously transformed by technology and other social forces. In the short term, this implies that children meet grade-level standards so that they can move through elementary and middle school and arrive at high school ready to tackle college-preparatory mathematics. These standards, in school systems throughout the country, are not necessarily consistent or coherent. They are sometimes driven by a "back to basics" mentality. For example, in Chicago students must pass a statewide test in sixth grade in order to be promoted. They are sometimes driven by a goal of "world class" standards. For example, President Clinton recently announced a goal for all students to complete algebra by eighth grade and that national progress toward this goal be measured by a test resembling the Third International Mathematics and Science Study test.

I also believe that mathematics literacy implies, in the long term, that students complete higher-level mathematics courses in high school and arrive at college ready to take college-level mathematics for college credit (instead of being recycled through developmental mathematics courses as a prerequisite to further college study). Although there is also debate about what this mathematics education should look like in high school, it is clear that there is a foundation of study that gives students access to a broad range of career opportunities. Further, mathematics is playing a much broader role in gaining access to these opportunities.

In the National Council of Teachers of Mathematics elaboration of curriculum, assessment, and evaluation standards, there is an important attempt to recognize that all students can and should use mathematics as a natural part of learning (NCTM 1995, 1989). This is described in the idea of mathematical power. Mathematical power includes the ability to apply mathematical knowledge to solve problems, the ability to use mathematical language to communicate ideas, and the ability to reason and analyze. In addition a positive disposition toward the value of mathematics is needed. I believe it is essential in the mathematics education of African American children to impart mathematical power. To be mathematically literate is not only to have knowledge but also to be able to use it.

An equally important goal is that mathematics have sociocultural relevance for students. This is particularly important if mathematics learning is understood to involve some type of constructive activity that draws on the experience of students—experiences defined by a local community or sociocultural group, experiences defined by their peer groups, or experiences created in the classroom. For example, in the curricular materials of the Algebra Project founded by Robert Moses, students construct make-do stories or stories where in their experience they have had to substitute one item for another. These stories are used to introduce students to the idea of equivalence. It could also be suggested that students' generational experience and facilities with certain forms of technology give them a different cultural context for understanding and doing mathematics. It is also important to make clear that mathematics is part of a broad African American cultural tradition. For more information, the Louisiana State University Library has an extensive Internet Web site on African Americans in the sciences (www.lib.lsu.edu).

I also believe that critical historical and social factors must be addressed when setting goals for the mathematics education of African American children. For example, according to Moses et al. (1989, p. 437):

> Many children of color learn from an early age that there are doubts concerning their capacity to develop intellectually. Messages communicated from school

(low ability placements in the primary grades), from peers (pervasive anti-intellectualism within the peer group), and the media (expectations of inferiority) all serve to impress upon them that they may not be up to the task of advanced studies. The lack of confidence engendered by the internalization of these messages shapes the meaning of any failure ("I guess this proves I'm not smart") and undermines the capacity to work ("Why bang my head against the wall if I'm unable to learn the stuff anyway?").

Claude Steele has also recently suggested a form of stereotype vulnerability that hinders the work of African American students (Steele 1992).

It is paramount in the mathematics classroom that teachers work to restore children's self-confidence, their capacity to self-assess and develop independent and collaborative learning strategies, and a sense of efficacy—that feeling of assurance that work in learning mathematics will pay off. This goal is also essential if it is accepted that the immense work of systemic school reform is just beginning. It is necessary to be aware that the next mathematics classroom a student walks into may not have a mathematics educator who is competent or believes that African American children can learn. Students must have skills that will allow them to negotiate schools and classrooms that do not have consistent expectations.

I also believe that mathematics educators of African American children must see mathematics education reform in a broader set of social goals. Again, social and historical forces have led to a system of schooling that might be said to marginalize African American children. Failure of students to gain mathematics literacy will only increase this marginalization. However, this problem cannot be solved just in an individual teacher's classroom. Although the classroom is the primary arena of teaching and learning for a classroom teacher, it is only a part of a greater community that has an impact on the classroom, as well as being influenced by what happens in the classroom. Sometimes the problems of the community can overwhelm the functioning of a school.

Whereas traditionally, schools narrow community involvement to encouraging parents to support their own children, I believe teachers must have a more expansive view of the impact of their work. For example, Moses (1994, p. 110) provides a view of the social issues involved in achieving mathematics literacy, gained from his work in the 1960s organizing African Americans in Mississippi to gain voting rights:

> In my view, many people will see our vision [of mathematics literacy] as impossible. There's a sense in which most people are not going to believe or accept any of this agenda until they are confronted with the products of such an effort: students who come out of schools and classrooms armed with a new understanding of the mathematics and with a new understanding of themselves as leaders, participants and learners. How do classrooms get transformed into places where students can develop in these ways?... Part of what

happened in Mississippi was the creation of a culture of change—a change in the climate of the consciousness of Black people in that state. Part of what was involved was tapping into a consciousness. The vote provided a consensus. Everyone agreed that if they could get the vote, it would be a good thing, and they would be better off. So we could rally people across a wide spectrum to work together. I think the same window of opportunity is available around the issue of mathematics literacy. I think everyone agrees that if it is possible to open the door to real mathematical understanding, it would a good thing, and we would all be better off.

This may seem far from what a mathematics educator may see as an educational goal, particularly a goal that influences evaluation and assessment. However, I believe that if the question of achieving mathematics literacy and giving students the capacity to learn and navigate through schools in our current social context is relevant to educators, then how their work meshes with a larger community of individuals who have a stake in schools is essential. I believe two goals address these broader social issues and can be directly tied to classroom work: (1) the demonstrations for school stakeholders, including parents, other teachers, and students, that mathematics literacy can be achieved; and, (2) the development of students who become advocates for their own mathematics education.

I'm sure that many other goals could be added to this list. At least at this stage, criteria can be set regarding the purpose of assessment and evaluation. Setting these criteria it should serve to give us information about efforts at achieving these goals. From the perspective of classroom teachers, assessment and evaluation should yield information about what students are learning, how they are learning, and how work in the classroom is building a greater community of support. However, before going further, it will be useful to clarify and define some of the technical issues surrounding the idea of evaluation and assessment.

Evaluation and Assessment: Some Technical Definitions

Michael Scriven gives us a broad and commonly accepted definition of the term *evaluation*. "The key sense of the term 'evaluation' refers to the process of determining the *merit*, *worth*, or *value* of something, or the product of that process. Terms used to refer to this process or part of it include: appraise, analyze, assess, critique, examine, grade, inspect, judge, rate, rank, review, study, test...." (Scriven 1991, p. 139). In Scriven's view, assessment is synonymous with the term *evaluation*. It has been suggested that the term *assessment* can be used more narrowly to identify the process of collecting information up to the point of making an evaluative judgment. I shall assume that the terms *evaluation* and *assessment* are essentially interchangeable words for the same process. Consequently, I am beginning with the

idea that classroom teachers, in assessing their students, are looking for information that is valuable for understanding the teaching and learning environment that is being created in their classrooms.

The value of assessment also depends on the purposes for which it is being collected and is closely connected to the different audiences that may use or demand assessment information. "Who is assessing whom? For what reason? Assessment is an attitude before it is a method. And in elementary classrooms there are three quite different attitudes or stances that teachers adopt with respect to monitoring and evaluating children's learning" (Chittenden 1991, p. 29). Chittenden discusses several attitudes that guide teachers' work—keeping track, checking up, and finding out for the school district, parents, themselves as teachers, or the students. He notes that although these stances are basically complementary, they can be in conflict. A clear case of this problem is the attention teachers pay to preparing students for school-wide standardized tests (Lomax et al. 1995). Although such tests play an important role in defining issues of accountability, it is difficult to understand what role these tests can play in the immediate work of classroom teaching. Test results come in months after the test, making them useless for any ongoing teaching decisions with any particular child. There is also clearly a need to understand what we are keeping track of, checking up on, and finding out about, and to answer the question, What is valuable or worthwhile to assess?

Attached to an assessment attitude or stance are methods. These methods can be understood as ways of gathering evidence or assessment data. It may be surprising that a list of types of evidence that can be collected is rather short. Direct observation of students' behavior, tests and testlike results (paper and pencil or direct questioning), and samples of performance (work products and other artifacts) are the primary sources of evidence. In current discussions about assessment, evidence that comes either from direct observations or from evaluating samples of students' work have been linked with the idea of alternative assessments (Webb and Coxford 1993). In table 1 an excerpt from an NCTM publication illustrates how purpose, audience, and type of assessment method might be understood (NCTM 1989, p. 200).

This table provides some logical connections between assessment methods and assessment purposes. If we want to know what students understand about a mathematical procedure, we should ask students to explain their procedure. But what type of answers actually give us useful information about students' understanding of the procedure? Is there a particular set of questions that we should ask to "draw out" students' understanding? When can we say we have truly made an assessment of students' understanding?

Technically, these issues involve specifying the reliability and validity of an assessment method or instrument. An instrument is reliable if, when reapplied, it produces the same data or result. An instrument has validity if it measures what

Table 1
Purposes and Methods of Assessment

Purpose (examples of questions asked)	For Whose Use	Unit of Assessment	Type of Assessment	Assessment Methods
Diagnostic				
• What does this student understand about the concept or procedure?	Individual teacher	Individual student	• Tasks that focus specific skill, type of procedure, concept, strategy, or a type of reasoning	• Observation • Oral questions that ask students to explain their procedures
• What aspects of problem solving are causing difficulty?	Individual student		• Each student evaluated	• Focused written tasks
• What accounts for this student's unwillingness to attempt new problems or see the application of previously learned materials?				• Directed test items

it is intended to measure. A standardized test, in this context, has uniform instruction for it's administration, use, scoring, and interpretation. This standardization is an attempt to improve reliability. The test may also be designed to produce data that are normally distributed because it is assumed that the intention is to measure mathematical knowledge, which is normally distributed (a bell-shaped distribution where there is an average amount of mathematical knowledge that most individuals acquire, with fewer numbers of individuals scoring higher or lower than the average). These normative criteria for the results of the assessment method are then used as evidence of validity. However, it does depend on a particular view of what we are evaluating.

Alternative ways of thinking about validity have emerged under the label of *authentic assessment*. "In the wake of the concerns about standardized measures, individual teachers, districts, and states are developing new kinds of testing measures based on entire performances. Currently taking the form chiefly of portfolios and performance-based tasks, these measures are often referred to as authentic assessment; and they are designed to present a broader, more genuine picture of student learning" (Zessoules and Gardner 1991, p. 49). Of course, the meaning of the notion of a genuine picture of student learning that gives authentic assessments their validity must still be made explicit. What do we look for in a portfolio of students' work? It would be safe to assume that what is valued in a genuine picture of student learning is quite different from what is valued in a normative comparison of one student to some group, which is the foundation of some norm-referenced tests.

The reliability and validity of an assessment instrument is not just a technical problem. It depends on some underlying beliefs and assumptions. I think a critical issue for teachers of mathematics is understanding the types of interpretations that can frame assessments. Ultimately, the usefulness of an assessment depends on the match between what an assess-

ment is intended to measure and a teacher's beliefs and assumptions about what is being assessed.

Dimensions of Mathematics Learning and Assessment

In my work I have found it useful to think about different understandings and beliefs about mathematics and science learning along four dimensions (Davis 1990). These dimensions have their roots in philosophical and psychological theory about the structure of knowledge and the behavior and capacities of human beings who acquire knowledge. These dimensions are based on Stephen Pepper's (1942) theory of world hypotheses. Pepper characterized world hypotheses as overarching hypotheses about the structure of reality and consequently the nature of knowledge. These hypotheses are not simply a system for categorizing philosophical arguments about knowledge. Rather, they are products of an ongoing process of the acquisition of knowledge and, consequently, are still subject to elaboration and proof. In world hypotheses we should see trends and schools of thought that continue to be refined and extended in scope in the contemporary world.

In order to construct his theory, Pepper had to make some assumptions about what it means to acquire and have knowledge. He assumed that knowledge could be defined as a system of beliefs ranging from common sense knowledge to highly refined knowledge. This range of knowledge is a consequence of different types of evidence that might be used to support one's beliefs. Uncriticized evidence corresponds to commonsense knowledge; criticized evidence corresponds to refined knowledge. In Pepper's view, this range of evidence implied a uniquely human process of knowing that seeks to move from uncriticized to criticized evidence. This process that leads to criticized evidence must involve two types of corroboration: structural corroboration, which is the corroboration of "fact" with "fact" (although this does not imply that a "fact" can be identified), and multiplicative corroboration, which is the corroboration of individuals with individuals.

Through structural corroboration, Pepper asserted, all knowledge must emerge and be constructed within a relational structure where one piece of evidence is tied to another in some type of collaborative way. Relational structures give knowledge cohesiveness. Different types of relational structures result in exclusive systems of knowledge that Pepper called world hypotheses.

How does a relational structure develop that supports structural corroboration? Pepper proposed that this development could be represented by the construction of metaphors, where in various ways one meaning or structure is applied to another by analogy. Structure built by analogy underlies much of what we call factual knowledge. For each world hypothesis, Pepper identified a root metaphor that he believed captures its historical and continuing development.

There is one more essential process in the process of acquiring knowledge. Occurring simultaneously with a process of structural corroboration is a process of multiplicative corroboration. Through multiplicative corroboration, which is the corroboration of individuals with individuals, all knowledge acquires an interpersonal dimension. In essence, all knowledge must have the possibility of common agreement. The possibility of multiplicative corroboration is as much a part of the possibility of criticizing evidence as structural corroboration is.

Consequently, when we look at a history of knowledge, we observe the interplay of structural and multiplicative corroboration. In Pepper's view, we observe a process where greater and greater structural webs of evidence are constructed. These webs explain a collective reality with increasing precision and scope. The largest of these structures are world hypotheses. Pepper proposed that four hypotheses have reached the status of world hypotheses: formism, mechanism, contextualism, and organicism.

Although these dimensions can be taken as boundary lines for broad debates among conflicting theories, they all have some commonsense kernel of truth, at least in our contemporary state of knowledge. Although each would accept a paper-and-pencil test of mathematical knowledge and skills, each dimension would have a very different way of interpreting results. Each has a prescription about how teaching and learning may best be carried out. Each has a point of view about how basic mathematics skills should be taught as well as higher-order mathematics. Each has implications about how learners are viewed and, in some instances, what social forces shape their school lives. The *worth*, *merit*, or *value* assessed and the reliability and validity of the assessment make sense only within these understandings and beliefs.

Dimension 1

Mathematics as a logical structure that reflects a reality of quality and relationships among qualities, acquired through abstract thought. The elements of mathematics (number, line, point, greater than, equality, etc.) appear to support the existence of certain qualities and relationships among qualities that define abstract or universal forms. These forms either have some type of real existence or are imposed on our experience because of the structure of our mind. From a "commonsense" point of view, the observation of similar objects (an extreme example might be a picture of a sheep and its clone) could easily lead to an inference of the existence of universal forms and laws that describe the transformation of forms that are at work in nature. This dimension in Western philosophy has a long history and is often emphasized by mathematicians who see mathematics embodied within an objective and independent reality, or a reflection of the human mind's capacity to structure phenomena through logic and abstraction.

This dimension gains support from other disciplines. In physics, the search for fundamental physical laws, such as laws about symmetry that explain and constrain relationships among fundamental subatomic particles, relies on this view. In the world of biology, the definition of a living entity by a genetic code that reproduces itself guides much contemporary research. Although life depends on a hospitable environment, its form depends on laws that are virtually independent of environment.

This dimension implies that an essential component of learning involves abstract conceptualization and reasoning. A process of learning must be able to detect patterns and similarities and to construct qualities and relationships that explain these patterns. In this dimension the best way to think of a mathematics curriculum is that it lays out a conceptual map of mathematical knowledge as well as rules that show how the map can be built logically. In this framework, assessment and evaluation must have, as primary objectives, the measuring of students' conceptual maps of mathematical knowledge and their ability to build and extend this knowledge through abstract thinking.

I believe that this dimension supplies the foundation for those who wish to rely primarily on standardized tests to assess students' knowledge. One aspect of the validity of these tests comes from agreement on the domain of mathematical knowledge students should know at any particular point in their mathematics education. A more controversial aspect of validity comes from assumptions about the capacity for abstract reasoning. For example, following biologists who see a genetic code as specifying similarities and differences in the human form, some psychologists have proposed that there is an innate, genetically determined capacity to reason abstractly that is not dependent on individual or social experiences. (Arthur Jensen [1969] and more recently

Hernstein and Murray [1994] argue that intellectual capacity is an inherited genetic trait. Their theory depends on being able to associate variability in IQ with variability in life outcomes. However, the work is premised on the particular assumption that there are aspects of human forms that obey laws virtually independent of concrete experience.) If intellectual capacity is distributed in a particular way, then the results of the application of this capacity (mathematical knowledge) will also be distributed in the same way. Consequently, for those taking this position, an assessment should display this normative criterion if it is to be accepted as a valid and reliable measure. (There are more benign psychological explanations offered that might find their way into validity arguments within this dimension. For example, Howard Gardner's [1993] theory of multiple intelligence might also be used to establish a normed view of what to expect when we test for mathematical knowledge.)

It is important to note that not all tests are built with the underlying assumptions of this dimension. The National Assessment of Educational Progress (NAEP) tests draw their foundation from the NCTM *Standards*, claiming to measure several different "strands" of knowledge (number sense, properties, and operations; measurement, geometry, and spatial sense; data analysis, statistics, and probability; and algebra and functions), as well as several mathematical abilities (conceptual understanding, procedural knowledge, or a combination of both in problem solving) and mathematical power (Reese et al. 1997). The assessment also does not produce a comparison of a student to some normative idea of how all students will perform. Instead, it defines students as performing at a basic, proficient, or advanced level. The validity of this test depends on a definition of different levels of competence that should be achieved by all students, and its value lies in establishing a way to assess progress toward particular goals. However, it is not difficult to imagine someone applying a different interpretation and, when reading that certain groups do not perform as well as other groups, taking this as evidence that students need to be put on different tracks so that the talented can proceed unencumbered by those who do not have the capacity for mathematics learning.

Dimension 2

Mathematics as a generalization of a concrete world, acquired through concrete experience. In this framework, there is a very strong sense that mathematics must be directly tied to an individual's concrete experiencing of phenomena. The commonsense analogy that frames this dimension is the operation of a machine. The machine could be explained if all its parts and connections were visible. Assuming that there are no spiritual agents moving reality for a purpose, then we must imagine ourselves as parts of a massive cosmic machine. Any knowledge that we have must be derived from its effects, whose qualities are inferred through our senses. Ultimately, our experiences in this machine are the basis for all learning. Numbers, points, lines, and other mathematical entities are probably complex linguistic signs recording the consequence of behaving in certain ways. For example, children can construct signs and symbols about equality and inequality from manipulating groups of concrete objects or construct an idea about equivalence by manipulating weights on a balance.

This dimension is reflected in the contemporary work of physicists who search for a vast quantum electromagnetic gravitational field that may indicate the work of a cosmic mechanism. A biologist working from this point of view may work on understanding the principles of molecular biology where DNA and interrelations between RNA and other biochemical agents define the genetic makeup and reproduction of living entities. They may further note that when one places these living mechanisms in an environment, a larger mechanism must be explained that defines an ecology in which species may live or die.

Learning in this dimension must be explained from the physical and concrete phenomena of human experience. There is a long history of individuals trying to build a psychology of learning that fits into this dimension, notably represented by behaviorists, such as B. F. Skinner (1981). Typically, behaviorists and psychologists who want to talk about human behavior need to assume some type of motives or needs (rewards or avoidance of punishment) that drive behavior and have consequences that may direct behavior toward certain ends. Over time, the consequences of a history of behaviors is encoded in knowledge and skills, and even into identifiable personality traits. For example, mathematics anxiety might be associated with individuals whose experience in learning mathematics is accompanied with extreme discomfort.

In addition, with enough study, a set of experiences and conditions that lead to a behavioral repertoire that represents competence in mathematics at various levels may be understood. Maybe some of this repertoire is assumed to occur before formal schooling in the social environment of the family. For those missing these types of experiences, we might propose a "head start" program.

In this dimension, mathematics is understood as a complex system of signs and relationships among signs that mark the consequences of behaviors over time. A mathematics curriculum is built by identifying observable behaviors that delineate mathematical skills: the ability to manipulate and identify numbers by counting, the ability to apply procedures that solve word problems, the ability to create mathematical theorems, and so on. These behaviors might be defined into a set of competencies that build on one another. For example, an individual who is learning how to solve algebraic equations must be competent at adding and subtracting integers. This understanding of competence may even get encoded into a computer software package that automatically moves a learner through a set of experiences and decides on the basis of a set of indicators that the learner is ready for a new learning experience.

Assessment in this perspective involves measuring competence. This competence can involve having appropriate knowledge needed to carry out a task. However, observable behavior that illustrates the mastery of a task is the target of assessment. In this instance, a criterion-referenced test, or a test that is built on an external standard of proficiency, is more appropriate than a norm-referenced test, and direct observation of mathematical performances may be more desirable. Validity in this dimension is intimately tied to an understanding of the set of behavioral activities that compose a competency and the conditions under which such behaviors can be elicited. Assessment, in fact, can serve as important feedback to a learner about the mastery of all the skills needed to complete a task. An assessment can be a reinforcement for acquiring desired behaviors.

In addition, in this dimension it is relevant to consider other aspects of behavior that may affect performance, including a history of learning that may affect learners' motivations and expectations about successful performance. Affective components of behavior are an important component of learning.

Dimension 3

Mathematics as a reflection of an inner structure of thought guided by the need to remove contradiction in an experienced reality. The previous two dimensions have defined mathematics from some type of basic building blocks: either (1) a system of qualities and relationships among qualities that give us various mathematical forms or (2) signs and symbols built up from an experience. This dimension looks at mathematics from the perspective of an inner process of human development. (Looking back, we find that mathematical knowledge, as well as other types of knowledge, appears to develop in stages. These stages tend to move toward more accuracy and coherence, a higher stage explaining what appeared to be contradictory in a lower stage.) This type of development requires some type of overarching process that focuses learning on the problem of achieving more coherent states of knowledge.

The commonsense idea that frames this dimension is the development of a biological organism. A biological organism emerges in stages, with each stage incorporating and responding to developments in the previous stage but having a more coherent organization. There is some type of self-regulative process that directs biological growth. Using biological growth as a metaphor for the growth of knowledge seems reasonable.

A physicist who embraces this perspective would emphasize that scientific knowledge is more than a state of knowledge about an independent reality. It is a stage of knowledge that has developed and will continue to develop through the resolution of conflicting conceptions of scientific phenomena into more consistent and ordered models of reality. For example, an important problem in understanding the fundamental laws of physics is integrating a description of gravitational force with nuclear and electromagnetic forces. A uniform conception of force would create a more consistent and ordered description of reality. However, the resolution of this problem will undoubtedly lead to new conceptual confusions and contradictions, setting the stage for further refinement and growth of scientific knowledge. In general, the growth of scientific knowledge (and possibly all knowledge) is toward a more coherent, consistent, and accurate description of reality.

These ideas about the development of knowledge imply that the process of learning must involve some type of continual reflection on what has been learned and the need to identify and resolve contradictions. Learning can be identified with a process of reflective abstraction. Furthermore, if the notion of biological growth is correct, a psychology of learning may also involve understanding different stages of mental growth, where the structure of thought itself changes. Children's ways of thinking will be different from adults' ways of thinking. This approach is clearly illustrated in the work of Jean Piaget (1971). Piaget defined a sequence of mental stages that emerge from a learning process embedded in an organic process of self-regulation. He called the learning process "reflective abstraction," representing an inner psychological self-reflection and abstraction of physical and, eventually, mental activity. In his view, all knowledge is constructed within, and framed by, cognitive structures that themselves develop as a result of learning. In Piaget's (1971) terms, a philosophical conception of knowledge requires the construction of a genetic epistemology.

It is important to note that this dimension is also used to support developmental theories about both the cognitive and the affective aspects of life. The development of an ego is often associated with the redefinition of a self with an outside world because of imbalances caused in experience (Kegan 1982). The self (or ego) develops by building more coherent and consistent ways of interacting, typically moving from an egocentric view of the reality to a self-autonomous perspective. One of the difficulties in this line of thinking is that all development has to be explained from the inside. Even learning is essentially an inner regulated process. Outside agents, such as teachers, can only facilitate change. They cannot qualitatively change how it will occur.

Mathematics in this dimension is intimately tied to stages of mental development as well as to an accumulating collective history of mathematical knowledge. Mathematics reflects a history of learning that has produced contradictions, whose resolutions result in more coherent and consistent knowledge. In this context, a mathematics curriculum should reflect two types of subject matter: subject matter that actually changes the nature of thought and subject matter that expands the content of thought. For example, a child learning how to solve algebraic equations is simultaneously applying operations of thought involving inverse and reversible operations as well as modeling some concrete situation in an equation. If a child's mental structures do not allow reversible operations, it will be impossible for the child to have full access to algebraic knowledge. Learning mathematics involves reflective abstraction.

An assessment in this dimension serves several purposes, including to identify a child's current stage of mathematical thinking or ideas about some mathematical content, to assist a child in focusing on and seeing contradictions in his or her thinking, and to assist a child in constructing mathematical ideas that are more coherent and consistent. Assessment should primarily provide an opportunity for children to do reflective abstraction. The validity of any assessment would depend on building a case that an accurate picture of the way a child is thinking has been captured. Possibly, an analysis of the types of systematic errors of thinking would be a component of establishing validity.

In this dimension, assessment evidence should reveal what a child is thinking about, so that a teacher can facilitate—possibly by asking questions, by clarifying perceptions, or by introducing a new context for thinking—in order for the child to do the self-reflection and abstraction that would result in new knowledge and possible new structures of thought.

Dimension 4

Mathematics as socially constructed knowledge that serves human purposes. Mathematics is clearly a very important tool in problem solving and human experimentation that has transformed reality. It has been developed in a social, as well as physical, reality that requires collective and individual adaptive learning activities. An individual who learns mathematics is acquiring a set of instrumental tools that have been found collectively to be useful for human purposes.

The commonsense notion that underpins this dimension is the need to impose a human context in order to explain an event. It is difficult to describe or construct meanings about events without the specification of a context. For example, the construction of meanings about the desegregation of schools will be quite different in a context involving the distribution of school resources versus a context about children experiencing teaching that respects cultural diversity. Or in mathematics, it is easier to conceptualize equality in a context—or the concept of equivalence—than to abstract an all-encompassing concept of equality. In essence, the construction of meaning or understanding about experiences always emerges in a context that is infused with human and socially imposed purposes and intentions.

In physics, this dimension can be aligned with elements of quantum mechanics where the properties of a system that attempts to measure phenomena (the observer) cannot be separated from the phenomena themselves (the observed system). This has led some physicists to suggest that an explanation of reality through a description of a mechanism or through a formal system of laws of physics is impossible. In socioeconomic studies, the line of thought associated with Marxist philosophy begins with an assumption that the instrumental and necessary activities of labor frame all human relationships and knowledge. In this context, the basic economic method of exchange (capital) carries with it a set of instrumental social relationships that can either benefit or hinder individuals. Over time, societies build institutions (e.g., schools and prisons) reflecting collective knowledge and a system or relationship that has developed through the basic activity of labor. These institutions may reflect unequal relationships of power and restricted access to capital. Recently, this type of analysis has been applied to those types of social skills that enhance success in schools (e.g., ability to use accepted school discourse, ability to use powerful adults to one's advantage, ability to manipulate school resources to solve problems). These skills are a form of social capital (Stanton-Salazar 1997). Through learning in their home, communities, and schools, children acquire various amounts of social capital.

Mathematics in this view is a socially constructed body of knowledge developed to address unique human problems. Mathematics learning can be associated with human problem solving and experimentation. A difficult aspect of this dimension is that in learning mathematics, children need to construct mathematical ideas as they relate to their own and others' intentions and purposes. The latter include a history of learning that has already produced a body of knowledge with social conventions. For example, a child who is learning about the meaning of zero on a number line may have to see this number as a solution to a problem about recognizing a benchmark. This benchmark may represent the absence of some quality (ratio scale) or simply a relative position between qualities (interval scale). These decisions involve socially constructed ideas about reality that are embedded in many of the procedural rules about mathematics, and they need to be reanalyzed in a current problem situation. Learning mathematics is much like learning a language, which has signs and symbols that carry social meaning and that in the purposeful activity of discourse are reconstructed and possibly changed.

Assessment in this dimension can also involve testing for certain mathematical knowledge and procedural skills. However, the validity of an assessment must be drawn from a broader notion of how this knowledge is grounded in a context. For example, testing a student's understanding of the expression $8 - 10 = -2$ would involve examining whether a student understands the expression as a problem about comparison where the difference can be expressed as a number that has both magnitude and direction and where the meaning of the magnitude and direction is embedded in various contexts with agreed-on convention involving what numerical quantities measure. In learning about such numbers, a student must construct an idea or have a hypothesis and be able to test, verify, and explain these ideas in a social reality.

Dimensions of Learning and Assessment: In Retrospect

I have found these four dimensions to be useful in thinking about mathematics learning and what we may be attempting to evaluate or assess in a classroom. It is important to note that none of these dimensions is "neutral." Each dimension presents a view of what is learned in mathematics, how learning occurs, and what essential features of learners and their social environment may affect the learning process. Each dimension presents a frame for understanding and interpreting reliability and validity in an assessment or evaluation. Each can be the setting of debate about what is an adequate philosophy of mathematics. (Thomas Tymoczko [1985] and John Dossey [1992] have written about a history of competing philosophies of mathematics and the continuing effort to construct philosophies adequate for the needs of contemporary mathematicians and mathematics educators.) These debates continue in many forums, probably because no one position can totally subsume the others, and each carries some semblance of "common sense."

system of assessment and evaluation, then teachers have no way to assess the effect or value of their work. I believe these dimensions provide at least a map of the type of interpretations that can be made. In table 2, I have summarized how each of these dimensions defines mathematical knowledge and learning and how assessment data would be interpreted or can be said to have reliability and validity. We next need to see what the implications of these various dimensions are for defining assessments that address the goals for the mathematics education of African American children.

Relating the Dimensions of Mathematics Learning and Assessment to the Goals for the Mathematics Education of African American Students

I hope it is clear that attempting to make distinctions about assessment methods is impossible without considering how they acquire validity and reliability within our assumptions about what is learned and how learning occurs. Although in some instances measurement tools are

Table 2
Dimensions of Mathematics Learning and Assessment

Dimension 1	Dimension 2	Dimension 3	Dimension 4
• Mathematics as a logical structure of qualities and relations	• Mathematics as generalization of concrete experiencing	• Mathematics as a reflection of an inner structure of thought	• Mathematics as socially constructed knowledge
Learning mathematics requires abstract conceptualization.	Learning mathematics requires concrete experiencing.	• Mathematics learning as reflective abstraction	• Mathematics learning as problem solving or experimentation
Assessment involves evaluating the level and depth of conceptual mathematical knowledge. Reliability and validity depend on students' ability to conceptualize mathematical phenomena through logical thinking. If this type of thinking is itself distributed in some type of normative way, an assessment should display this distribution among groups of students.	Assessment involves determining behavioral competence. Reliability and validity depend on creating the conditions for measuring mathematical behaviors. An assessment should lead to an understanding of where a student may be along a trajectory of behavioral experience that will lead to competence. Assessment is essential for determining the next steps.	Assessment involves evaluating a current stage of cognitive development, and the implication of that stage for having coherent and comprehensive mathematical knowledge. Reliability and validity depend on having accurate products of children's thinking. Assessment should help to identify ways to facilitate further mental development.	Assessment involves evaluating students as they develop, test, verify, and explain ideas and hypotheses. Reliability and validity involve understanding the context in which students construct and solve problems.

In my work, I find that many teachers accept different definitions about what is being taught and how it should be taught, depending on goals that they believe are important and the immediate situations in their classrooms. However, if teachers cannot match classroom goals—and strategies and beliefs about what is needed to achieve these goals—to a

designed to directly reflect underlying assumptions about what is being measured (normed standardized tests and elaborate scoring rubrics for performance assessment), many assessments are not particularly the on-the-spot classroom assessment that a teacher may do to make an immediate instructional decision.

The simple act of examining a student's work on a "drill and practice" worksheet is open to various interpretations. In fact, it is difficult to condemn worksheets without understanding what value a teacher attaches to the work and, consequently, how it is used in an instructional strategy. For example, if a student had been independently working on a solution to a problem and with the teacher's help was able to identify that the lack of some type of basic mathematics computation skill was an obstacle, then work on that skill might be important and valuable for to enable the student to achieve the solution to the problem.

In table 3, I have summarized my assumptions about goals for the mathematics education of African American children against the various dimensions of mathematics learning and assessment. I have indicated which dimension might provide valuable information and guidance in achieving particular goals. I believe this is the starting point for any teacher to begin to develop more formally a set of appropriate assessment tools for classroom work.

The term *mathematical literacy* has been used to describe what African American children should achieve. Each of these dimensions appears to provide a valuable interpretation of what this literacy involves. The assessment of current conceptual understanding, of expected competencies or the mastery of skills, of the current stage of mathematical thinking or the ability to define and solve problems—all are valuable in regard to the goal of achieving mathematical literacy.

Dimension 4 offers a way for teachers to deal with the seeming contradiction of having to teach "basics" instead of skills that open up mathematical power. The "basics" are clearly a part of the accepted language of mathematics and are an essential part of the tools mathematics provide to decipher and construct meaning. It is a critical task for students to align this language with their systems of mathemati-

cal meaning. However, experimentation with the construction of mathematical meanings that solves problems does not have to be limited by a knowledge of accepted rules and meanings Through their invented systems of mathematics, children can still struggle with important mathematical concepts and, more important, begin discussions with others about their mathematical ideas.

It is again important to note that dimension 1 is used to suggest that not all students have the capacity to learn mathematics. Either implicitly or explicitly, in the notions of ability groupings or tracking, it is used to cut off access to higher-level mathematics. This is an implication that cannot be simply dismissed, since there is a strong "commonsense" idea that individuals do have some type of unique potential that simply unfolds through a life cycle. It is a condition of our current society that race and class are seen to be the indicators of this potential, rather than skills or knowledge associated with the activity itself.

The impact and role of sociocultural experiences on mathematical knowledge, however, does not have equal importance in all dimensions. Dimensions 2 and 3 suggest that the experiences in which students either build competent mathematical performances or resolve inner contradictions are very important, although in dimension 3 a knowledge of these experiences is important only for accurate assessment of a child's thinking. Sociocultural experience plays a more central role in dimension 4 because students' construction of meaning, and their intentions in experimentation and problem solving, are believed to emerge in their sociocultural experience and be a key to learning.

In contrast, the broad definition of mathematical power almost requires aspects of each dimension. Mathematical power includes the ability to apply mathematical knowledge to solve problems (all dimensions), the ability to use mathe-

Table 3
The Relationship between Assessment Goals and Dimensions

	Goals	Dimensions			
		1	2	3	4
Subject Knowledge	Mathematical literacy	*	*	*	*
	Sociocultural relevance		*	*	*
Student	Mathematical power	*	*	*	*
	Attitude and disposition		*		*
	Efficacy		*		*
Community	Demonstration that mathematical literacy can be achieved	*	*	*	*
	Student-advocates for mathematical literacy				*

matical language to communicate ideas (dimension 4), and the ability to reason and analyze (dimensions 1 and 3). It also requires having a positive disposition toward the value of mathematics (dimensions 2 and 4). Dimensions 2 and 4 clearly embrace the importance of positive attitudes toward mathematics either by setting mathematical behavior into a system of motives and needs or by attaching learning to particular human purposes and intentions.

Efficacy can be associated with an orientation toward experimentation and problem solving. Key to dimension 4 is the capacity to sustain an effort to construct and question ideas and to negotiate meaning with others. A reasonable expectation is that learners will internalize this role that they play in acquiring new knowledge. In addition, it might be expected that students who build an increasing repertoire of competent mathematical behavior will develop a sense of overall mathematical competence (dimension 2).

Finally, all dimensions can be used to demonstrate that mathematics literacy is being achieved in the classroom. However, dimension 4 provides a way of thinking about empowering students. It is in this dimension that the social implications of mathematics learning are most clearly shared with students.

Next Steps in Building Better Assessments

A quick perusal of table 3 illustrates that there are several choices that can be made in defining assessments across various goals—and these choices have implications about the validity and meaning of any evidences that are collected. I believe the next steps for a teacher would be to make decisions about how best to consistently assess and evaluate students. In this context, some dimensions appear to offer more possibilities than others for meeting the current challenges of mathematics education for African American children.

I do not want to suggest that this is an easy task or that decisions can be made that eliminate working across various dimensions. It is not difficult to imagine that the task also gets harder if it requires the agreement of a large number of educators about what should be assessed. For example, it has become clear that the apparatus needed to do large-scale performance assessment is very expensive, primarily because the assessment requires sophisticated evaluation of performances and procedures to ensure the evaluation is done in a reliable way (Stecher and Klein 1997). In this context, the path of least resistance is the typical multiple-choice standardized test.

However, in the classroom, where there are multiple goals that require ongoing assessment decisions, teachers must take on the task of selecting appropriate assessment strategies and understanding these strategies in relation to their beliefs and teaching practices. In my work with program evaluation, we typically start a project by having extensive discussions with the project planners and implementors

about their goals. We also ask about their theories of action or their beliefs about what type of activities will actuate their goals. It is only after these ideas are explicitly understood that an evaluation design can be constructed where there is a clear understanding of what data will be collected and how they will be interpreted. The assessments that are performed would be useless if they could not address the goals and the ideas about how these goals are being achieved.

Classroom teachers are, in a sense, simultaneously program planners, implementors, and evaluators. Because of their complex role, assessment must "make sense" to them to be of use. This was part of what was described as the "bottom line." I believe an important step is for teachers to grapple with the different ways that mathematics and mathematics learning can be framed and therefore the different ways we explain the validity and meaning of assessments. It may actually relieve teachers to see that there are different ways in which the mathematics learning process can be cast.

It is also clear in many discussions about successful teachers of African American children that they do teach in a way that not only meets many goals but also recognizes that each child must be seen as a whole person. For example, Gloria Ladson-Billings (1994), in a conception of culturally relevant teaching, suggests that effective teaching requires in-depth knowledge of the subject as well as in-depth knowledge of the child, and Jacqueline Irvine (1991, p. 119) has stated that "effective teachers of minority students often develop idiosyncratic styles of teaching and relating to their students." These teachers appear to be aware that success depends on (1) having an array of goals that encompass subject matter, the student, and the context of schooling and (2) having a way to monitor the success and failure of their classroom work.

Finally, Lisa Delpit (1995, p. 46), in the context of debates about teaching writing through a "skill" versus "process" approach notes:

> In conclusion, I am proposing a resolution for the skills/process debate. In short, the debate is fallacious; the dichotomy is false. The issue is really an illusion created initially not by teachers but by academics whose worldview demands the creation of categorical divisions—not for the purpose of better teaching, but for the goal of easier analysis. As I have been reminded by many teachers since the publication of my article, those who are most skillful at educating black and poor children do not allow themselves to be placed in "skills" or "process" boxes. They understand the need for both approaches, the need to help students establish their own voices, and to coach those voices to produce notes that will be heard clearly in the larger society.

Similarly, teachers of mathematics must use multiple perspectives in assessing and facilitating the mathematic voices of their students.

References

Chittenden, Edward. "Authentic Assessment, Evaluation, and Documentation of Student Performance." In *Expanding Student Assessment*, edited by Vito Perrone, pp. 22-31. Alexandria, Va.: Association for Supervision and Curriculum Development, 1991.

Cooney, Thomas J., Elizabeth Badger, and Melvin R. Wilson. "Assessment, Understanding Mathematics, and Distinguishing Visions from Mirages." In *Assessment in the Mathematics Classroom*, 1993 Yearbook of the National Council of Teachers of Mathematics, edited by Norman L. Webb, pp. 239-47. Reston, Va.: National Council of Teachers of Mathematics, 1993.

Davis, Frank. "Assessing Science Education: A Case for Multiple Perspectives." In *The Assessment of Hands-on Elementary Science Programs*, edited by George Hein, pp. 95-111. Grand Folks, N. Dak.: North Dakota Study Group on Evaluation, University of North Dakota Press, 1990.

Delpit, Lisa. *Other People's Children: Cultural Conflict in the Class Room*. New York: The New Press, 1995.

Dossey, John. "The Nature of Mathematics: Its Role and Its Influence." In *Handbook of Research on Mathematics Teaching and Learning*, edited by Douglas A. Grouws, pp. 39-48. New York: Macmillan Publishing Co., 1992.

Gardner, H. *Frames of Mind: The Theory of Multiple Intelligences*. New York: Basic Books, 1993.

Herman, Joan L., Pamela R. Aschbacher, and Lynn Winters. *A Practical Guide to Alternative Assessment*. Alexandria, Va.: Association for Supervision and Curriculum Development, 1992.

Hernstein, Richard, and Charles Murray. *The Bell Curve: Intelligence and Class Structure in American Life*. New York: The Free Press, 1994.

Irvine, Jacqueline. *Black Students and School Failure: Policies, Practices, and Prescriptions*. New York: Praeger Publishing, 1991.

Jensen, Arthur. "How Much Can We Boost IQ and Scholastic Achievement?" *Harvard Educational Review*, Reprint No. 2, pp. 1-123, 1969.

Kegan, Robert. *The Evolving Self: Problems and Process in Human Development*. Cambridge, Mass.: Harvard University Press, 1982.

Ladson-Billings, Gloria. *The Dreamkeepers: Successful Teachers of African American Children*. San Francisco, Calif.: Jossey-Bass Publishing, 1994.

Lomax, Richard G., Mary M. West, Maryellen C. Harmon, Katherine A. Viator, and George F. Madaus. "The Impact of Mandated Standardized Testing on Minority Students." *Journal of Negro Education* 64 (1995,2): 171-85.

Moses, Robert, Meiko Kamii, Susan Swap, and Jeffrey Howard. "The Algebra Project: Organizing in the Spirit of Ella." *Harvard Educational Review* 59 (1989): 423-43.

Moses, Robert. "Remarks on the Struggle for Citizenship and Math/Science Literacy." *Journal of Mathematical Behavior* 13 (1994): 107-11.

National Council of Teachers of Mathematics. *Assessment Standards for School Mathematics*. Reston, Va.: The National Council of Teachers of Mathematics, 1995.

———. *Curriculum and Evaluation Standards for School Mathematics*. Reston, Va.: The National Council of Teachers of Mathematics, 1989.

Pepper, Stephen. *World Hypotheses: A Study in Evidence*. Berkeley, Calif.: University of California Press, 1942.

Piaget, Jean. *Biology and Knowledge: An Essay on the Relation between Organic Regulations and Cognitive Processes*. Chicago, Il.: University of Chicago, 1971.

Reese, Clyde M., Karen E. Miller, John Mazzeo, and John Dossey. *NAEP 1996: Mathematics Report Card for the Nation and the States*. Washington, D.C.: National Center for Education Statistics, 1997.

Scriven, Michael. *Evaluation Thesaurus*. 4th ed. Newbury Park, Calif.: Sage Publishing, 1991.

Skinner, B. F. "The Science of Learning." *Harvard Educational Review*, Reprint Series No. 15 (1981): 77-87.

Stanton-Salazar, Ricardo D. "A Social Capital Framework for Understanding the Socialization of Racial Minority Children and Youths." *Harvard Educational Review* 67 (1997): 1-40.

Stecher, Brian, and Stephen Klein. "The Cost of Science Performance Assessments in Large-Scale Testing Programs." *Educational Evaluation and Policy Analysis*, 19 (1997, 1): 1-14.

Steele, Claude. "Race and the Schooling of Black Americans." *Atlantic Monthly* 269 (1992, 9): 68-78.

Tymoczko, Thomas. *New Directions in the Philosophy of Mathematics*. Boston, Mass.: Birkhauser, 1986.

Webb, Norman L., ed. *Assessment in the Mathematics Classroom*, 1993 Yearbook of the National Council of Teachers of Mathematics. Reston, Va.: National Council of Teachers of Mathematics, 1993.

Zessoules, Rieneke, and Howard Gardner. "Authentic Assessment: Beyond the Buzzword and into the Classroom." In *Expanding Student Assessment*, edited by Vito Perrone. pp. 47-71. Alexandria, Va.: Association for Supervision and Curriculum Development, 1991.

When the Vision Confronts Reality: Implementing Reform in Elementary School Mathematics in an Urban School District

Patricia F. Campbell
University of Maryland

I am going to discuss a project that has been in place for more than one year in Baltimore City Public Schools (BCPS), in Maryland. This is a National Science Foundation–funded project in the Teacher Enhancement Division, supported under the Local Systemic Change (LSC) program. As such, this project is committed to catalyzing systemic reform in elementary school mathematics across the school system.

To offer some background, BCPS enrolls approximately 112 000 students, of whom 82 percent are African American and 70 percent qualify for free or reduced-fee lunch. There are approximately 2000 elementary school classroom teachers in BCPS, distributed over 122 elementary schools, of whom about 1700 teach mathematics in any given year. There is a high-stakes, statewide mathematics assessment in Maryland called the Maryland State Performance Assessment Program (MSPAP). Children are tested in third, fifth, and eighth grade on reading, writing and language arts, social studies, science, and mathematics, with high school testing looming on the horizon. The mathematics component of the assessment is grounded in the *Curriculum and Evaluation Standards for School Mathematics* of the National Council of Teachers of Mathematics (1989). Schools whose scores are low and indicate no improvement over time are deemed "reconstitution eligible." These schools must file improvement plans for state approval and show subsequent achievement gains or face "take over" by the state or a third-party agent of the state.

Given the reality of high-stakes testing, a performance assessment seems like a reasonable option. However, life in urban centers is rarely simple or consistent. Because of legislative concerns and lawsuits, a recent budget agreement authorized an additional appropriation of $254 million over five years to BCPS, with the conditions that (*a*) a standardized test be regularly administered to monitor achievement (probably the California Test of Basic Skills/Level 5), (*b*) the school board and the superintendent resign, and (*c*) the school system be reorganized under the guidance of a new Board of School Commissioners appointed by the mayor, the governor, and the state superintendent of public instruction. Massive changes at the top of an organization inevitably influence personnel and decision making, and school districts are not exempt—nor are the mathematics reform efforts within them.

The prior mathematics achievement levels within the system have been dismal. For example, of the 41 schools with whom our project is currently working, 26 are reconstitution eligible. One of my favorite quotations is from Louis V. Gerstner, Jr., the chief executive officer of IBM, who said, "No more prizes for predicting rain. Prizes only for building arks." You have come here to address possible approaches for building arks. I don't think that we have an ark yet, but we are in the process of launching what we hope will be a flotilla of serviceable rafts.

One Approach to Building a Raft

Collaboration

Mathematics: Application and Reasoning Skills (MARS) is a collaborative effort between the University of Maryland and Baltimore City Public Schools. The decisive word is *collaborative*, not cooperative. In this project, there are two

The research reported in this material was supported by the National Science Foundation under Grant No. ESI 9554186. The opinions, conclusions, or recommendations expressed in these materials are those of the author and do not necessarily reflect the views of the National Science Foundation.

45

organizations, the university and the school district. Other initiatives may presume the involvement of other organizations, such as a community group and a school or perhaps faculties from two schools. But in any event, committed personnel from each organization who respect one another's strengths, who accept one another's weaknesses, who reflect common perspectives or beliefs, and for whom the project represents a mutual sense of purpose are essential. In addition, the individuals must be willing to share success and failure. Although every person involved in the reform effort will not have this degree of focus, there must be a core of individuals for whom this is true. Reform efforts should be jointly planned by the individuals who share this level of conviction, with open lines of communication permitting flexibility.

A School-Based Model

MARS concentrates on curriculum revision and instructional reform within a school-based model as a means of addressing students' achievement. The assumption behind the model for MARS is that the necessary unit for change in mathematics teaching and learning is the school (Wideen 1992). It is difficult to achieve a school-based model, but the goal is to involve every teacher of mathematics from the participating schools. There are two reasons for this. First, there can be only one mathematics program in a school if students are to have a coherent, meaningful mathematics instruction over time. Second, it is very difficult for most isolated teachers to change their instructional practices, much less those isolated teachers in urban schools who are coping with constraining social and environmental conditions. When teachers from a school enter an enhancement effort together, they are able to share and address the constraints that exist within the culture and context of teaching in their particular community. A school-based model is not easy to implement, but it is potentially more powerful.

Curriculum Revision

With the publication of the NCTM *Standards* documents and the Maryland state mathematics performance outcomes, a supplement was developed to augment the BCPS mathematics curriculum. However, weaknesses remain. In particular, although the curriculum lists all the aspects of mathematics that are to be addressed each year in each grade, there is no sense of emphasis, of what pieces are more important. Furthermore, there are no guidelines for pacing or timing, leaving instructional implementation subject to high inconsistency, low expectations, and reduced opportunities for learning across classrooms. As a result, the curriculum is being revised again, using input from our national advisory board, from principals, and from our leadership teachers. The challenge is to have it ready by the beginning of the 1997 school year.

Instructional Model

MARS has a clear theoretical perspective regarding learning and instruction. In particular, the project clearly promotes the perspective that students actively construct their knowledge rather than passively receiving it (Noddings 1990). However, whereas instruction must build on and recognize a student's prior knowledge, the premise in MARS is to expect and support the mathematical understanding of each child.

Because the school district has a tradition of prescribed lesson plan formats, teachers originally expected and wanted to have a format for MARS. As a result, we developed a general guide for organizing instruction addressing motivation, analysis by the student and mathematical interaction with questioning form the teacher, followed by student reflection and sharing, again accompanied by the teacher's questioning. The emphasis during instruction is on understanding, conceptual development, problem solving, and student explanation and verification supported by the teacher's "judicious telling" (Chazan and Ball 1995, p. 18). Practice is addressed through homework and, potentially, after-school centers.

Professional Support and Enhancement

The model for teacher enhancement in MARS assumes a two-year commitment as teachers advance from awareness to understanding, to implementation, and toward continuing growth. During the first year, three leadership teachers from each participating school are offered a three-credit graduate mathematics education course through the University of Maryland, tuition-free. The leadership teachers agree to attempt instructional change in their classrooms and, possibly, to serve as peer coaches for their colleagues in the future. In addition, these teachers are advocates for mathematics in their schools. Last year, I team taught this course with a faculty member from Morgan State University in Baltimore. The intention was to foster increased graduate opportunities in mathematics education for teachers in Baltimore after the life of the LSC grant.

Each cooperating school is also assigned a half-time Instructional Support Teacher (IST). The IST is an excellent classroom teacher from BCPS whose role is to support change, foster implementation, promote reflection, applaud efforts, and challenge further growth. During the first year of the enhancement, the IST works in the classrooms of the three leadership teachers and three other volunteer teachers to support instructional change. The IST also coordinates grade-level mathematics planning meetings on a biweekly or monthly basis. These planning meetings initially acquaint the teachers with the expectations of the curriculum and raise the notion that mathematics instruction may use cooperative groups, manipulative materials, and something other than the traditional teacher demonstration followed by student practice. The IST is an essential feature of the MARS model because instructional change at the school level is difficult to accomplish without site-based support. Thus, the selection of the IST is important. The IST must be a person who is perceived by the teachers as a knowledgeable leader with classroom credibility.

The summer following the first year of the program, every classroom mathematics teacher is encouraged to attend a fourteen day, paid, in-service program. This staff development addresses (*a*) adult-level mathematics content; (*b*) teaching mathematics for understanding, including the use of manipulative materials, questioning, and focusing on the "big ideas" in the mathematics curriculum; (*c*) research on children's learning of some important mathematical topics peculiar to a grade range; and (*d*) implications for equitable teaching; in particular, examining one of the writings by Gloria Ladson-Billings (1990). The summer in-service program also includes a summer school program for children that provides teachers an opportunity to attempt instructional change with a small group of children without competing demands.

The intent for this summer program is for the teachers to begin classroom implementation, supported by their IST and their grade-level planning meetings. Throughout the following academic year, quarterly after-school workshops are held in four regions across the city, focusing on critical issues that have arisen within the program. These workshops are staffed by the ISTs. In addition, mathematics minicourses (eight 2-hour sessions) are offered at no charge for the teachers throughout the school year to foster the teacher's own mathematical content knowledge while offering the opportunity for state department of education credits that may be applied to certification renewal. These minicourses have been staffed by faculty at the University of Maryland for the past year, but the intent is to team teach these courses with faculty members from other institutions across the city of Baltimore in order to widen the base of local mathematics content–enhancement opportunities for teachers.

Administrative Support

Each fall, the project leaders hold a planning meeting with each cooperating principal, meeting the principal at the local school site. This meeting serves to clarify expectations, anticipate and minimize problems, and foster communication and cooperation. Subsequently, a principals' workshop held later in the fall addresses common misconceptions or concerns that have arisen at the local sites. A 1.5-day retreat is held each spring as well, and a two-day principals' conference is held each summer. Each local school indicates its support of the reform effort by financing one-sixth of an IST's salary and purchasing classroom sets of manipulative materials as well as revised commercial textbooks. In subsequent years, each of the local schools support an increasing share of the IST's salary.

Parent and Community Awareness

MARS has a parent and community component, but it is not yet fully implemented. Thus far, we have piloted an after-school parent-child program using multicultural literature as a context for mathematical problem solving. Pairs of teachers from participating schools have completed an in-service module where they learned how to work with adults and mixed-aged children in a setting where a multicultural story is read aloud by the teacher, with comprehension questions addressing both the literature and the underlying mathematical content. The caregivers and their children then work collaboratively to solve mathematical problems, guided by the teachers' questions. The intent is to provide caregivers with a model for discussing literature and managing read-aloud settings as well as a better understanding of the new approaches for learning and teaching mathematics. The teachers who enroll in the in-service module must agree to conduct six after-school parent-child sessions in their local school. The teachers receive a stipend for both attending the in-service module and conducting the sessions. During the pilot program, the grant assumed the cost of the literature books, which were supplied to each school. In the future, that cost must be assumed by the schools. The in-service module furnishes lesson plans for both the read-aloud comprehension segment and the subsequent mathematical problem-solving session.

Do the Rafts Float?

The Model

The simple answer to this question is, "Yes, but we keep having to plug up new leaks." We have not changed the basic design of our model; however, there are detractors within the school system and within the city who find the two-year model a convenient target. The desire to "fix" the schools is so great that fast, quick models are more appreciated. We are using a two-year approach in order to establish evidence in each building, prior to the summer in-service program, that teaching for understanding can take place in the classrooms of that school. In many urban schools, low expectations abound, often voiced in the refrain, "Not my kids! My kids can't do that!" Unfortunately, our experience this year has been that although some leadership teachers became models for their peers, others did not. However, because of our persistent belief that it is necessary to support curriculum awareness prior to instructional change, we are not changing the model at this time. We really do not know if the two-year approach yields greater eventual implementation, because we are just getting ready to enter our first full implementation year.

The Curriculum

The BCPS elementary grades mathematics curriculum for 1996–97 was actually found in three different documents that teachers needed to coordinate: the original curriculum guide, the supplement to address the revised state performance outcomes, and a third document that categorized the units of instruction according to their "big ideas." This "big idea" document was developed by MARS in an effort to limit the segmentation and short-term focus that seemed to characterize the teachers' planning efforts. Unfortunately, in most instances, the desired coordination between the three curriculum documents did not happen. As indicated earlier, the curriculum is currently being revised, and the challenge is to finish it before to the start of the coming school year. This effort is being "supported" by the district's interim administrator, who has determined that all curricula will be revised, with the first quarter's curriculum revisions being available by September 1997. The advantage of this joint revision process is that it will ease the passage of a curriculum revision through administrative channels. The disadvantage is that it is unlikely that any elementary school teacher can simultaneously address revisions in every content area. It is our hope that the IST's presence will make a difference since it is likely that teachers will attempt to address some curricular reform. Which one is the issue.

Supporting Teacher Change

Instructional "change is a process, not an event" (Fullan with Stiegelbauer 1991). For teachers, the instructional reforms being addressed in MARS represent a fundamental pedagogical shift. It is not easy to learn how to listen to children's explanations and to understand the intent or the mathematical implication of what a child has just shown or said. "Teachers must learn how to interpret children's responses to gain the information that is needed to develop or modify future instruction and to define questioning strategies to foster or challenge the understanding or misconception that is being revealed by individual children" (Campbell and White 1997, p. 326). During the past year, we have slowly learned that not only is it important to support the teachers in their efforts to change, but it is essential to try to characterize for principals what might occur in the classrooms in their schools as teachers engage in the reform effort. As a result of administrators' workshops or retreats, we have begun to address the kinds of inevitable half-steps or missteps that might characterize teachers' instruction as they attempt to implement reform. We do so in an effort to support the principal's role as the educational leader in the building. The intent is to characterize teachers' efforts as indicators of growth rather than as signs of failure. Simultaneously, our hope is to engage principals in discussion of how they might support their faculty's continued growth so that missteps are minimized. For example, many teachers have traditionally corrected a child's error by telling the correct answer. That is, many teachers view their responsibility as being one of "setting the child straight." In MARS, teachers are asked to consider the perspective of making instructional decisions in light of a child's reasoning

and of simultaneously supporting a child's future efforts to figure out a solution independently or to persist in the face of challenge. Consequently, many teachers adapt their teaching approaches when faced with an incorrect response from a child. Instead of telling a child, "No, that's wrong," teachers ask children to explain how they obtained a particular solution without telling the children that their solutions are in error. If a child self-corrects, everyone is happy. If a child does not self-correct, many teachers initially may not know what to say or do. In fact, many teachers initially respond, "Good thinking," and then simply call on another child, as if the error never happened! Although this is not the goal of our pedagogical approach, it seems to be an inevitable step in the process of instructional change.

As the teachers in the MARS program develop more expertise and interact with the IST and with other teachers in grade-level planning sessions, they begin to ask questions focusing on or confronting the child's erroneous reasoning. But in the meantime, an observer may decide that in MARS, or in any reform effort, there are no wrong answers—that whatever a child says is correct. Although communication is always a means of confronting rumor and myth, educating the school administrators about our instructional model is not easy, since urban elementary school principals are very busy people who find it difficult to fit in one more meeting. Nevertheless, our efforts to inform administrators of the model during three administrator conferences have been met with positive reviews. Many principals are eager to understand the instructional model and to support its implementation.

Teacher Enhancement

The greatest variability in the MARS implementation is the biweekly grade-level planning sessions. In about seven schools, they occur as planned every other week in every grade. Across the remaining schools, grade-level planning either happens once a month with all teachers (three schools), biweekly with some grades but not all grades (sixteen schools) or monthly with some grades but not all grades (eleven schools). In three schools, there are grade-level planning meetings, but they are held when the IST is not present. In one school, there is no grade-level planning. During the summer administrators' conference, this issue was addressed at some length. Unfortunately, those schools with the least opportunities for grade-level planning are the same schools whose principals were absent from the administrators' conference. Because the principals have been involved in the redesign of the curriculum format and organization, they are now more knowledgeable of the MARS curriculum and its changes. Furthermore, the school district's new push to revise the curriculum and to make principals responsible for its implementation has raised the stakes. We are hopeful that this system-wide interest in curriculum revision, coupled with the teachers' own increased understanding of MARS as a result of the summer in-service program, will yield a greater call for grade-level planning in the schools in the fall.

If attendance is a measure of success, then the summer in-service program was quite a hit. There were 327 teachers and 210 children present, despite soaring temperatures. Praise was frequent, and spirits were generally high. Although we administered both belief surveys and evaluation forms to the teachers, no effort has been made yet to examine or interpret the findings.

The Challenge of Reform

Little is really known about instructional change in urban settings. In MARS, we readily admit that we do not have all the answers. But we also clearly state that the current status of mathematics instruction is inadequate and that urban children are being limited by traditional educational practice. We ask our leadership teachers to work with us because together we can define a new paradigm for elementary school mathematics instruction in BCPS. Our ideal is to engage both teachers and principals in a school-based effort to define a new mathematics program that will expand instructional expertise and successfully engage all students in the power of mathematical work. It is too early to know if MARS is successful. But we must recognize that reform cannot only be situated in idealized settings. The challenge we must each accept is to expand and maintain the commitment to reform and educational growth across schools, including urban schools. There are many times when this effort is frustrating and the obstacles seem daunting. That is why it is important to have a shared sense of purpose with conviction. For me the source of that conviction is simple. It is in the eyes of the children—children who have, and more important, who know they have, mathematical power.

I want to share with you the image of such a child. When things get rough, remember this child because there are literally thousands of them in the urban and rural schools across this nation. At the time this problem solving interview was videotaped, this child was a second grader, and it was January. The child had had instruction on double-digit place value and on the meaning of subtraction. The child had not yet dealt with subtraction with regrouping in his class. *[Transcription of videotape follows.]*

Teacher: *[A paper with the problem 42-25 = ___ is placed before an African American male child. There is space below the horizontal problem. The child has a pencil.]* This time, (child's name), if you'd like, you can use these things. If you want to. *[Base-ten blocks are put within reach of the child.]*

Child: *[The child draws an arc under the problem connecting the 4 in 42 and the 2 in 25.]* Okay, so this is … 2. *[Writes 2.]* The first number's going to be 2 … and the next number's going to

be 1. *[Writes 1 yielding the answer 21 to the horizontal problem 42-25.]* … 21. Here, let me do it this way. *[Writes 42 in the space below the problem.]* … 25. *[Writes 25 above the 42 and draws a horizontal line under the 42. The child has written the problem 25-42 vertically.]* … These numbers have to be switched. *[Points to the 5 and the 2 in the ones column.]* Cause that's the way 3. *[Subtracts 5 minus 2. Writes 3 in the ones column of the solution.]* … I don't get 3 this time! But I think it's best that this one's right. *[Points to the answer 21 in the horizontal problem at the top of the page.]*

Teacher: Okay. Can you show me 42 with the blocks?

Child: 42. *[Quickly selects 4 tens and 2 ones from the collection of base-ten blocks.]*

Teacher: Now show…. Use these 42 *[indicating the blocks]* and show me minus 25. How do you subtract 25?

Child: *[Child removes 2 tens.]* Okay, so I took away 2 and here's 5. *[Puts his finger on the middle of the one remaining ten block.]*

Teacher: Okay. So what'cha got left?

Child: *[Child counts the remaining units on the ten, counting up from the placement of his finger on the ten and continues to count the other loose ones.]* Uh? Let me check this over again.

Teacher: Okay.

Child: This is, huh. This is how much I have. *[Picks up the remaining blocks and recounts.]* This would be…. *[Lays the 17 remaining blocks down and rearranges his position at the table.]* The answer is … is 17? *[Puzzled voice]*

Teacher: 17? Okay.

Child: I think. That's how I counted this. It's 17.

Teacher: That's how it…. Okay. How did you get rid of … *[interrupts self]*…? I saw you take the 20 over there…

Child: So let me look at this again.

Teacher: Okay, go ahead.

Child: So which number would you put first, the bigger or smaller?

Teacher: I'd put the one that came first, first.

Child: 42. *[Writes 42.]* Then minus 25. *[Writes-25 under the 42 and draws a horizontal line. The child has written the problem 42-25 vertically.]* But, this still doesn't make sense. 2 take away is 3. *[Writes 3 in the ones column.]* And this time, here is 2. 23. *[Writes a 2 in the tens place. His problem reads 42-25 = 23, vertically.]*

Teacher: So what did you get on the blocks?

Child: 17.

Teacher: 17. But you got a different number with the … the writing?

Child: Yeah.

Teacher: Hmmm.

Child: And each time. I think these two numbers are going to be the same. *[Points to the 3 in the ones column in the two vertical problems.]* But this one's different. *[Points to the 1 in the answer 21 for the horizontal problem at the top of the page.]*

Teacher: Okay. Okay. *[Repeated louder, signaling an end to this problem.]*

Child: Which one was right?

Teacher: Uh?

Child: Do you think this one's right, the cubes?

Teacher: What do you think?

Child: I think the cubes.

Teacher: You think the cubes were right. Okay.

Child: Maybe. *[Spoken very softly.]*

Teacher: Okay. Let's do something else now. *[Begins to remove the blocks.]* That was a lot of thinking, wasn't it? *[Continues to remove the blocks. Picks up the paper from in front of the child.]*

Child: So, I think the answer was 17.

Teacher: *[Lays the paper back in front of the child.]* Do you want to put that on there so I can remember? Why don't you put it here? *[Points to space above the answer 21 in the horizontal problem at the top of the page. Scratches out the 21.]*

Child: *[Writes 17 above the scratched-out 21.]*

Teacher: Thank you. *[Draws a circle around the answer 17.]* I'll put a circle on this so I can keep this straight. *[Removes the paper and reaches for the pencil.]*

Child: Okay. 17 plus 25.

Teacher: What's 17 plus 25?

Child: 42! *[Smiles broadly.]* Here, let me see that! *[Jumps up from his seat and reaches across the table for the base-ten blocks.]* I'm going to check out 17 plus 25.

Teacher: Okay.

Child: *[Takes 17 base-ten blocks, choosing 1 ten and 7 ones.]* There's 17 *[takes 25 base-ten blocks, choosing 2 tens and 5 ones]* and 25. *[Recounts the 5*

ones in the display of 25.]* Make sure that was 5. So let me see what else I'm going to get. 1, 2, 3, 4, 5, 6, 7 *[counting the 7 ones in 17]*, 17, 27, 37, *[pointing to the single ten in 17 and then the two tens in 25]*, 38, 39, 4-…. Uh, I went up 'stead of down!

Teacher: Well, you were adding 25 plus 17, right, to check it out?

Child: Yeah. So, let me do this again. *[Repositions the blocks into a set of 17 and a set of 25.]* I think 17's going to be the right answer.

Teacher: Okay.

Child: But let me just check. 17, 25, *[checking the positions of the two sets]* 25, 35 *[pointing to the set of 25 and then to the single ten in 17]* 36, 37, 38, 39, 40, *[moving ones from the set of 17 as he counts]* 17 was the right answer! *[Said joyfully with confidence.]*

This child's performance is not unique. For this child, and all the children like him, we must do more. This is work that must be done now. Remember, the character of the child is not the issue; the issue is the character of the instruction.

References

Campbell, Patricia F., and Dorothy Y. White. "Project IMPACT: Influencing and Supporting Teacher Change in Predominantly Minority Schools." In *Mathematics Teachers in Transition*, edited by Elizabeth Fennema and Barbara Scott-Nelson, pp. 309–55. Mahwah, N.J.: Lawrence Erlbaum Associates, 1997.

Chazan, Daniel, and Deborah L. Ball. "Beyond Exhortations Not to Tell: The Teacher's Role in Discussion-Intensive Mathematics Classes." Craft Paper 95–2, National Center for Research on Teacher Learning. East Lansing, Mich.: Michigan State University, 1995.

Fullan, Michael, and Suzanne Stiegelbauer. *The New Meaning of Educational Change.* New York: Teachers College Press, 1991.

Ladson-Billings, Gloria. "Culturally Relevant Teaching: Effective Instruction for Black Students." *College Board Review* (Spring 1990): 20–25.

National Council of Teachers of Mathematics. *Curriculum and Evaluation Standards for School Mathematics.* Reston, Va.: National Council of Teachers of Mathematics, 1989.

Noddings, Nell. "Constructivism in Mathematics Education." In *Constructivist Views on the Teaching and Learning of Mathematics, Journal for Research in Mathematics Education Monograph No. 4,* edited by Robert B. Davis and Carolyn A. Maher, pp. 7–18. Reston, Va.: National Council of Teachers of Mathematics, 1990.

Wideen, Marvin F. "School-Based Teacher Development." , *Teacher Development and Educational Change,* edited by Michael Fullan and Andy Hargreaves, pp. 123–55. Bristol, Pa.: Falmer, 1992.

Summaries of Discussions

Teaching and Learning Strand

Summary of Breakout Sessions on the Teaching and Learning of African American Students

Five groups of conference participants met to discuss the focus of plans for the Benjamin Banneker Association based on the presentation by Gloria Ladson-Billings. The discussion groups were led by Michaele Chappell, William Joyner, Howard Johnson, Gwendolyn Long, and Clara Tolbert. The groups suggested initiatives BBA should implement for parents, teachers, students—the entire community of learners. They also proposed organizational and professional actions BBA should take to benefit the education of African American students and to enhance the knowledge of the broader mathematics community.

Teachers' Role

Regarding the teaching and learning of African American children, participants stated that educators must provide a caring environment and exhibit professionalism so that children will learn "naturally." Teachers must respect humanity, hold high expectations, have the skills and commitment to teach all students, and most important, be culturally aware of students' individual backgrounds and experiences. Teachers of African American students must seek out peers who implement and model appropriate pedagogies, such as cooperative learning and culturally relevant approaches to mathematics learning. Basically, teachers need to develop an improved understanding of African American students and are obligated to share that knowledge with others.

Students' Role

Participants believe that students have an important role in their journey toward mathematical literacy and lifelong achievement. With our guidance, they must gain confidence in, and share responsibility for, learning mathematics. Students must place themselves within and value the learn-

ing process while simultaneously holding themselves to high expectations. To that end, students should be encouraged to participate in advanced mathematics classes and supported through that participation. BBA should also continue to encourage students through its awards programs and recognitions, but that encouragement should be extended by way of including students' voices within BBA publications. Partnering with students as well as other associations increases BBA's visibility, influence, and credibility.

The Association's Role

Support for students means the Benjamin Banneker Association's regional organizations must take on a larger role and embrace collaborative community involvement. BBA must have involvement that respects both the education of children and the input from the community that nurtures them. *Community* was defined at the conference to include parents, churches, social organizations, businesses, and other professional groups and organizations. In these collaborations, BBA can make use of the media to foster and increase respect for African American children and their learning. Specifically, BBA, through its members, should develop more formal mentoring programs for children, initiate parent programs that stress the importance of learning mathematics, encourage the community to get involved in appropriate assessment of their children's learning and the accountability of their schools, and demystify educational jargon to enable parents to become partners in the education of their children.

Generally, the consensus of conference participants was that BBA must become more *visible* and known in the profession as an effective educational partner. They stated that as a professional group, BBA should clarify its role in mathematics education by creating and disseminating position statements on the "pedagogy of poverty" and on mathematics as a "civil rights battleground." These documents and executive summaries must be distributed to BBA members, other professional organizations, teachers, and parents. BBA should use its newsletter, *The Banneker News*, to facilitate this increased visibility; for example, the newsletter could publicize updates on current research, furnish instructional materials for the classroom, announce mathematics competitions, and showcase student voices. Participants felt that BBA should strengthen its Web site and encourage the use of technology, especially the Internet, in student learning. Members of BBA agree that visibility in national and regional mathematics conferences is imperative if BBA is to be an influential voice in conversations on the learning and teaching of African American students.

In sum, the stakes are high when it comes to African Americans' learning and teaching. Supportive educational programs must be put in place for our children if we expect to raise expectations and standards. Without addressing African Americans' learning and teaching, there can be no discussion on policy and professional development. As BBA members, we accept the responsibilities that come with raising the educational standards for our children. We must make it happen.

And from a Participant... What Will It Take for "All" to Really Mean *All?*

Idorenyin Jamar
University of Pittsburgh

The Benjamin Banneker Association Leadership Conference has provided the opportunity for classroom teachers, school administrators, mathematicians, and university researchers to work together toward actualizing the organization's commitment "to finding solutions to the problems that must be solved in order for African American children to reach parity in opportunity to study and achieve in mathematics," as stated in the Benjamin Banneker Association brochure. I was pleased to have been given the opportunity to take part. As a university faculty member with the challenge of gaining tenure looming before me, it is sometimes easy to lose sight of the ultimate purpose of our work. I left the conference reinvigorated and strengthened by the sense of community, common purpose, and shared vision that permeated all the meetings and interactions. We must now seriously face the tasks that lie ahead.

The recent reforms in mathematics education, spearheaded by *A Nation at Risk* (National Commission on Excellence in Education 1983) and given form by the National Council of Teachers of Mathematics (NCTM) *Curriculum and Evaluation Standards* (1989), call for an expanded vision of what mathematics is, what it means to teach mathematics, and what it means for students to engage in mathematical activity. The *Standards* document also states that "all [emphasis mine] students need to learn more, and often different, mathematics" (p. 1). What will it take to make this inclusiveness a reality for African American students across the country?

There are many young people in our inner-city schools who are eager and willing to learn but who have been failed by the low expectations of some of those charged with their education. Being relegated to low-level mathematics courses and the endless repetition of basic skills, they are being "trained" at best for obsolescence and taught mathematical skills that are easily performed by the simple handheld calculator. As Secada (1989) cautions, systemic reform efforts will not automatically produce equity. Those who are *viewed* as deficient in mathematical skills will not be included in the reform process unless proactive efforts are made to include them.

Unfortunately, there are also many young people who see little connection between formal schooling and themselves, and though they may be physically present in the classroom, "not-learning" (Kohl 1994) has become their technique for coping. Too many African American, and other poor and minority students, fall into this category. Kohl (1994) cautions that we should not confuse "not-learning" with failure. "Failure is characterized by the frustrated will to know, whereas not-learning involves the will to refuse knowledge" (p. 6). When we talk about "all children," are we including these children? Do we feel that they can be reached, or do we, too, give up on them, blaming their environments for their "inability" to learn? This is a more serious, but equally important, challenge facing us. We cannot afford to lose so many who are on the brink of adulthood, who should be preparing to become productive contributors to their families and communities.

This discussion may seem to have taken a decidedly non-mathematical turn. However, it is clear that students will not learn mathematics if they have decided that school has nothing to offer them. We must clearly be concerned about the quality of the mathematics that they will have the opportunity to learn, but we must also be concerned about those whom our schools are not currently reaching.

There are many complex reasons for students' resistance and, ultimately, for their dropping out of school (Fine 1986). One reason stems from the fact that students become aware of the structural inequities within society that tend to perpetuate their condition. Fine raises an important issue (1986, p.407):

> Consider what would happen, in our present-day economy, to these young men and women if they all graduated. Would their employment and/or poverty prospects improve individually as well as collectively? Would the class, race, and gender differentials be eliminated or even reduced? Or does the absence of a high school diploma only obscure what would otherwise be the obvious conditions of structural unemployment, underemployment, and marginal employment disproportionately endured by minorities, women, and low-income individuals?

Ogbu (1986) advances a similar argument to explain why many "involuntary minorities" choose to resist efforts to educate them.

Such explanations would suggest that schools can do little to change this predicament. However, D'Amato (1987) points out that the situation is much more complex and clearly less hopeless. He documented a fact that is probably well known to classroom teachers: students may actively resist learning in one classroom and yet willingly, and effectively, participate in another. To add to Kohl's (1994) title, perhaps "I won't learn from you"—but I will learn from the teacher in the next room. I noticed this phenomenon as I conducted research in the classroom of a particularly well liked middle school mathematics teacher. As I sat in his classroom observing students working together on mathematical tasks, I was struck by the clear sounds of nonproductive chaos in the classroom next door. I finally asked the teacher about this and was informed that those were the same students that I had seen in his class the previous period, engaged in mathematics. I am still in the process of analyzing data from this research.

As I gradually came to understand, many things about this teacher made his classroom a safe and inviting place to become involved in mathematics. He and his students interacted comfortably with each other; he made mathematics accessible and understandable. He made it clear that he would do everything in his power to ensure that the students succeeded but that they had to meet him halfway.

D'Amato (1987) explains such examples of situation-dependent engagement with his notion of "rationale" for learning. He posits that most students will tend to rebel against the demands of school if they do not have a reason for expending the effort needed to engage in the learning process. For students from mainstream environments where the payoff for their efforts is taken for granted, a *structural rationale* provides the needed motivation. This grows from these students' conviction, based on the models that surround them, that academic achievement will have a direct impact on their future success. Other students may have personal experiences with few, if any, people who have actually benefited from schooling. Their experience is more likely to suggest that such efforts will not be rewarded, and other means

exist to make a living, which are not dependent on school achievement. For such students to engage in school learning, a *situational rationale* would have to be present. In this situation, the context of a particular classroom would determine whether or not the student chose to become involved, whether or not it was "hip" to choose intellectual excellence (Ladson-Billings 1994).

The Algebra Project (Silva and Moses 1990) and others (e.g., Strong 1997; Keynes 1995; Resnick et al. 1991) are examples of educational efforts that give a broad spectrum of inner-city students the opportunity to grapple with sound mathematical ideas and an environment in which such efforts are the norm. It can be done. What it will take for our mathematics classrooms to present opportunities for all children to take part in high-quality mathematical endeavors? First we must ensure that opportunities for learning exist. Prior failure to master basic skills must not be used as an excuse to limit students' access to deeper educational engagement. As we educators gain a better understanding of the necessary prerequisites for authentic involvement, we may find that contextualizing mathematics will open up many more avenues of access for children (e.g., the availability of calculators can compensate for gaps in students' skills [Strong 1997]). As mathematics takes on more meaning for them, students may be more willing to gain reasonable proficiency in those missing skills. Yet, we must also guard against efforts to camouflage substandard content through the use of impressive-sounding course titles (Silver 1997) and pedagogical options.

Second, we must work to better understand the more reluctant learner. As we learn more about the sociocultural influences on students' resistance to learning mathematics (Hart and Allexsaht-Snider 1996), we will be able to create mathematics classrooms that appeal to students' situational rationales. Notions of cultural congruence and cultural compatibility (e.g., Vogt, Jordan, and Tharp 1987; Foster 1989) focus on classroom features that make the learning environment comfortable and inviting to nonmainstream students and thus can be thought of as influencing students' situational rationales. Classrooms that are sensitive to such features (Jamar 1995) will be more successful for diverse learners, and mathematics taught in a way that validates and empowers students' thinking can serve to awaken students to their potential as learners.

Finally, it is not enough to create individual classrooms that work. Since it is difficult to have a systemwide impact, we have to find ways to move beyond situational rationales and find ways to have an effect on students' *structural* rationales. Students empowered in one teacher's classroom must come to understand that whereas another teacher might not appreciate their independence of thought, they should also understand that this should not become an excuse for "tuning out" in the classroom. We need to help students connect learning and intellectual engagement to their lives and their sense of what is possible. "Culturally Relevant Teaching"

(Ladson-Billings 1994), a concept that grew out of the research of the keynote speaker at our conference, moves into this domain. Although it is true that culturally relevant teachers create classrooms that engage even unwilling learners, these teachers go beyond to situate students within the broader social reality that they have come to understand. Furthermore, culturally relevant teachers help develop within that arena a space for "academic excellence" that didn't exist before (Ladson-Billings 1994). In the process, a new structural rationale may emerge that could provide a basis for engaging in learning that is consistent with the reality of the student's world and that could transcend any individual teacher's influence. This is not an easy task, but teachers concerned about such matters will likely continue to strive in this direction, confident that they have been able to make a difference in some young people's lives. We need to spread the word.

The Benjamin Banneker Association is in a position to help to move this agenda forward. As we progress as an organization and try to influence these issues on a national level, we must continually monitor the quality of the mathematics being taught in our inner-city schools and spearhead efforts to bring it up to standard. We should also draw on our collective expertise and experience to help the educational community better understand African American learners in the context of mathematics classrooms so that they can develop classrooms in which *all* students engage in significant mathematical thinking. Finally, we must realize that our responsibility to our students extends beyond mathematics. We must help them negotiate the difficult path to adulthood and discover the powerful role that learning and intellectual pursuits can have on their lives and on the future of their community.

"Nobody told me the road would be easy ...," the refrain of a popular gospel song, echoes through my mind as I close. Yes, these are difficult tasks, but perhaps as we think back about the road we have already traveled, we can draw on the strength of the multitudes whose struggles have brought us to this point and redouble our efforts with renewed vigor.

References

D'Amato, John. "The Belly of the Beast: On Cultural Differences, Castelike Status, and the Politics of School." *Anthropology and Education Quarterly* 18 (1987): 357-60.

Fine, Michelle. "Why Urban Adolescents Drop into and out of Public High School." *Teachers College Record* 87 (1986): 393-409.

Foster, Michéle. "It's Cooking Now: A Performance Analysis of the Speech Events of a Black Teacher in an Urban Community College." *Language in Society* 18 (1989): 1-29.

Hart, Laurie E., and Martha Allexsaht-Snider. "Sociocultural and Motivational Contexts of Mathematics Learning for Diverse Students." In *Motivation in Mathematics*, edited by Martha Carr, pp. 1-23. Cresskill, N.J.: Hampton Press, 1996.

Jamar, Idorenyin. "Teacher Support of Student Thinking in an Inner-City Mathematics Classroom: The Sociocognitive Dimension." Paper presented at the Annual Meeting of the American Educational Research Association, San Francisco, 1995.

Keynes, Harvey B. "Can Equity Thrive in a Culture of Mathematical Excellence?" In *New Directions for Equity in Mathematics Education,* edited by Walter G. Secada, Elizabeth Fennema, and Lisa B. Adajian, pp. 57-92. Cambridge: Cambridge University Press, 1995.

Kohl, Herbert. *"I Won't Learn from You" and Other Thoughts on Creative Maladjustment.* New York: The New Press, 1994.

Ladson-Billings, Gloria. *The Dreamkeepers: Successful Teachers of African American Children.* San Francisco: Jossey-Bass Publishers, 1994.

National Commission on Excellence in Education. *A Nation at Risk: The Imperative for Educational Reform.* Washington, D.C.: U.S. Government Printing Office, 1983.

National Council of Teachers of Mathematics. *Curriculum and Evaluation Standards for School Mathematics.* Reston, Va.: National Council of Teachers of Mathematics, 1989.

Ogbu, John U. "The Consequences of the American Caste System." In *The School Achievement of Minority Children: New Perspectives*, edited by U. Neisser, pp. 19-56. Hillsdale, N.J.: Lawrence Erlbaum Associates, 1986.

Resnick, Lauren B., Victoria Bill, Sharon Lesgold, and Mary Leer. "Thinking in Arithmetic Class." In *Teaching Advanced Skills to at-Risk Students: Views from Research and Practice*, edited by B. Means, C. Chelemer, and M.S. Knapp, pp. 27-53. San Francisco: Jossey-Bass Publishers, 1991.

Secada, Walter. "Agenda Setting, Enlightened Self-Interest, and Equity in Mathematics Education." *Peabody Journal of Education* 66 (1989): 22-56.

Silva, Cynthia M., and Robert P. Moses. "The Algebra Project: Making Middle School Mathematics Count." *Journal of Negro Education* 59 (1990): 375-91.

Silver, Edward A. " 'Algebra for All'—Increasing Student Access to Algebraic Ideas, Not Just Algebra Courses." *Mathematics Teaching in the Middle School* 2 (February 1997): 204-07.

Strong, Dorothy. "Algebra and Technology—a Powerful Team for a Class of Ninety Seventh and Eighth Graders." Paper presented at the 75th Annual Meeting of the National Council of Teachers of Mathematics, Minneapolis, April 1997.

Vogt, Lynn A., Cathie Jordan, and Roland G. Tharp. "Explaining School Failure, Producing School Success: Two Cases." *Anthropology and Education Quarterly* 18 (1987): 276-86.

Policy Strand

Summary of Breakout Sessions on Policy That Affects the Learning of African American Children

Five groups of conference participants met to discuss the focus of plans for the Benjamin Banneker Association based on the presentation of Steven Cox. The discussion groups were led by Harriet Haynes, Irvin Vance, Irene Outlaw, Arneita Jolly, and Jennie Bennett. The five groups focused their discussions on how policy decisions affect the mathematics education of students, especially African American students, and on the strategies that the Benjamin Banneker Association could implement to affect these policies. Participants agreed that the crucial, broad, educational policy issues that addressed appropriate and effective education for all students included tracking, testing, and standards-based educational practices.

Tracking

Participants believe that tracking obstructs the opportunity to learn mathematics for many students. Policies in place that support the tracking of elementary and middle school students as well as magnet programs in grades K–12 have created academically challenging mathematics classes for students who are *expected* to take algebra in the seventh, eighth, or ninth grades and have perpetuated remedial mathematics classes for all others. Participants stated that such policies stunt the growth of many African American students because most of the lower-track or special education students are minority students. Thus, tracking policies systematically do a disservice to African Americans. Additionally, only small numbers of African American children are recommended for academically gifted programs; these decisions concerning the mathematics future of children are often based on the recommendations of uninformed, unconcerned, or misguided school personnel. To address concerns about tracking and policies associated with it, the groups recommended that position papers be written, publicized, and disseminated. BBA should also examine magnet schools and special education policies for gifted and academically challenged children.

Testing

The Groups' concerns about testing policies at the national, state, and district levels were focused on the tests' structure, the incongruence between the tests' format and classroom experience, teachers' content knowledge, the evaluation of free-response test items, and the use of test data. Recommendations are for the development of position papers and for BBA to encourage (1) that staff development on test preparation and resource materials be made more available to teachers, (2) that teachers with strong content knowledge and pedagogical skills teach the sudents who are weak in mathematics skills, and (3) that mathematics teachers acknowledge and try to improve students' poor reading skills in mathematics.

Standards-Based Practices

Conference participants agreed that standards-based education is necessary for the mathematics learning of African American children. Groups acknowledged the work of the National Science Foundation (NSF) to develop standards-based mathematics materials that would provide a quality education for all children, but they also realized that money for these programs is often sparse in schools with large numbers of African American children. The NSF materials and other standards-based strategies require financial support from the school system for professional development, materials, and technology. Other problems with policy decisions related to standards-based education identified by the conference participants were the lack of understanding of parents and politicians, the prevalence of tracking in standards-based classrooms, and different levels of standards among local, state, and national initiatives. Groups recommended that BBA develop position papers on these issues and take organizational steps to expand BBA's influence.

Recommendations

Groups made strong recommendations to affect policy decisions. BBA should (1) encourage more members to participate in educational organizations and to become members of boards where policy is being made, (2) increase membership nationally, (3) network with other professional organizations, (4) orchestrate a national symposium, (5) be a voice in the making of policy that affects the mathematics education of North America's children, and (6) ensure its participation in policymaking so that *all* the stakeholders are "at the table" when policy is discussed and formulated.

Groups also suggested that BBA and its members get involved in policy decisions at the local level by establishing outreach programs for parents, working with schools having small African American populations, examining school climate, and developing mentor programs.

The overriding theme of the policy discussions was for BBA to develop strong positions related to policy decisions that affect the mathematics learning of African American children. Suggested topics for position papers included certification requirements opportunities to learn mathematics, teaching in urban settings, standards, curriculum, testing, tracking, and lifelong learning.

In sum, BBA members recognized the power that policy making provides. Members believe that by becoming an integral part of policy discussion and formulation, BBA's voice will be recognized, considered, and more important, heard.

Transforming Policy to Enhance the Lives of African American Mathematics Students

Jennie Bennett
Houston Independent School District

Policy decisions that affect the lives of mathematics students, especially African American students, are made daily at various levels. Decisions are made within the school and outside the school setting that affect not only students but curriculum, instruction, and assessment as well. In order for the United States to remain competitive in a global and technological society, efforts must be geared toward inclusion for all in mathematics. We live in a democratic society. Subsequently, barriers can no longer exist as obstacles for African American students' success in mathematics and enrollment in higher-level mathematics courses at the high school level. Equity for all requires challenge for all (National Research Council 1989); therefore, it is imperative that all mathematics educators accept the challenge of actively working to change policy so that more students of color, especially African American students, enter the pipeline of mathematics for success in school and life. Similarly, vigorous grass-roots efforts inside and outside schools should seek to end the tracking of African American students out of higher-level mathematics classes, such as advanced placement calculus.

In a report to the Rand Corporation, Hawkins (1995) identified barriers to mathematics opportunities in high school related to tracking:

> Minority access to high-track mathematics classes decreases as minority enrollment increases, i.e., as the proportion of minority students increased, the relative proportion of college preparatory or advanced course sections decreased. In a racially mixed school, minority students were more likely than their White peers to be tracked into low-level classes.

Since the National Council of Teachers of Mathematics (NCTM) published its *Curriculum and Evaluation Standards* document in 1989, many state and local education agencies have altered curriculum policy from "algebra for few" to "algebra for all." How can algebra for all become a reality for African American students?

Policy decisions by states and local school districts can provide all students with the opportunity to participate in algebra classrooms. Texas recently changed its high school mathematics curriculum to eliminate low-level mathematics courses. This policy change also includes an algebra strand in the grades pre-K–8 mathematics curriculum. When students enter Texas public high schools, the sequence of mathematics courses is algebra 1, geometry, algebra 2. If students opt to take four years of mathematics in high school instead of the required three years, they can enroll in AP calculus. However, students can no longer enroll in precalculus or calculus courses. Higher standards and expectations have been put in place as a result of offering only one option for students: AP calculus. Many middle schools in Texas are enrolling mathematics students in algebra 1 in the eighth grade. Subsequently, these students enter the ninth grade taking geometry with one more year of required mathematics courses to complete prior to graduation. These students take algebra 2 in order to meet the required standard of three years of high school mathematics. Realistically, if some students decide not to take AP calculus or a new course, Mathematical Models with Applications, they will take no mathematics at all.

As a result of these changes in Texas, not only will there be algebra for all, but geometry for all will also be emphasized. The best chance for this "algebra and geometry for all" notion to survive change is for mathematics educators, business people, and parents to work as a community of learners in order to establish goals and objectives that involve all students in algebra and geometry coursework. After all, community members have a vested interest in making sure that high-quality mathematics instruction is a reality for the children of Texas. No one has all the answers, but together, they can find the answers.

The process for change in the Texas mathematics curricula was spearheaded by a state mandate to revise the curriculum every eight years prior to textbook adoption. Philosophical positions and curricular decisions were based on research and the *Curriculum and Evaluation Standards for School Mathematics* (NCTM 1989). Discussions for a period of three years included designing a curriculum and setting standards that offered a mathematics program for all students, especially African American children. Curricular and pedagogical support for students as they engage in mathematical thinking and problem solving were included. The Texas mathematics curriculum documents emphasize the use of manipulatives and technology, together with an alignment to state mathematics assessment instruments.

More African American children in Texas will now have an opportunity to take higher-level mathematics courses that previously were not available to them. What comes next? Now that this new curriculum is being implemented, how can we ensure that children of color are in upper-level mathematics?

Parents can have an influence on policy! Banks and Banks (1993) state that some parents do want to participate in setting school policy, selecting curriculum materials, reviewing budgets, or interviewing prospective staff members. As mathematics educators, it is our responsibility to initiate opportunities for parents to be involved in decision making, as offered in the Comer School Development Program model.

The School Development Program, founded by child psychiatrist James Comer of Yale University, was first implemented in 1968 in the two lowest achieving schools in New Haven, Connecticut. Today 541 elementary schools, 107 middle schools, and 73 high schools are using the School Development Program, also known as the Comer Process.

Comer believes that many inner-city school-aged children come to school without the personal, social, and moral development necessary for academic success. To compound this problem, many school staff members lack adequate knowledge of child development and the children's home culture and are unprepared to deal adequately with the students and their families. Part of the success of the School Development Program can be attributed to Comer's nine-part process to improve the educators' knowledge of child development and to enhance healthier relations between school and home. Parent teams are designed to involve parents in all areas of school life.

When I directed the Marguerite Ross-Barnett Bridge Program at the University of Houston, I saw firsthand how parents can influence the tracking of their African American chil-

dren into higher-level mathematics. The goal of this year-round program was to filter middle and high school African American and Hispanic students of average ability into upper-level mathematics courses. Participants had to enroll in four years of high school mathematics, graduate from high school, and go to college to pursue a career in mathematics, the sciences, technology, or engineering. Both the child and the parent had to commit to the program from middle school through high school. Parents were required to attend parent-education workshops. Workshop sessions were designed to empower parents and their children with information necessary for the student's success.

Another program, the Bernard Harris Summer Science Camp, is designed for rising seventh, eighth, and ninth graders. In follow-up sessions, parents were given information about ways to ensure that their African American and Hispanic children were in mathematics classes that prepared them for college and life. Several parents reported that they had to challenge their children's high school counselor because the counselor placed these students in low-level mathematics classes other than algebra 1. When these parents confronted the counselor, they stated that the counselor told them that their children were not "college material." These parents insisted that their children be placed in an algebra class and upper-level mathematics because these youngsters were going to college in spite of the fact that they were economically deprived. As a result of the parents' actions, these students successfully completed algebra 1 and entered their junior year of high school still enrolled in mathematics classes. In fact, the students' appetite for learning mathematics increased. Parents reported that their children's self-esteem in mathematics improved. These parents made academic recommendations that would include their children in the arena of mathematics for all. Both parents and students felt empowered by their drive to enter and find success in the mathematics program. Clearly, it is of paramount importance that parents be educated so that they are able to serve as positive catalysts and advocates for improved mathematics education for all children, especially the unempowered majority of African American children. We need to involve these stakeholders, parents, in the decision-making process in order to alter the entrenched attitudes and practices of excluding African American and other children from the mathematics pipeline.

In summary, we must challenge the status quo that holds preconceived notions about African American students' mathematical ability. Action must begin with more than just reform rhetoric. Action must be filled with sound practices that ensure that African American students have the opportunities to possess the knowledge, skills, and beliefs necessary to become successful "doers" of mathematics today as well as in the future.

References

Banks, James, and Cherry Banks. *Multicultural Education: Issues and Perspectives*, 2nd ed. Boston: Allyn and Bacon, 1993.

Hawkins, William. *Constructing a Secure Mathematics Pipeline for Minority Students*. Math Research-Based Decision Making Series. National Research Center on the Gifted and Talented: University of Connecticut, 1995.

National Council of Teachers of Mathematics. *Curriculum and Evaluation Standards for School Mathematics*. Reston, Va.: National Council of Teachers of Mathematics, 1989.

National Research Council. *Everybody Counts: A Report to the Nation on the Future of Mathematics Education*. Washington, D.C.: National Research Council, 1989.

Implementing Policies for Urban Student Achievement

Clara Tolbert
Urban Systemic Initiative
School District of Philadelphia

Large cities with significantly large and diverse student populations do not find themselves with a large proportion of their young people achieving at high academic levels. For comprehensive educational reform to succeed in our country, it must succeed in our large cities. The School District of Philadelphia's *Children Achieving* action design charts a four-and-one-half-year course that will enable Philadelphia to be the first major city in the United States to meet this challenge.

Policies for Student Success

The action design is organized around the following ten components of the Children Achieving agenda and was adopted by the Philadelphia Board of Education in February 1995:

1. Set high expectations for everyone.

2. Design accurate performance indicators to hold everyone accountable for results.

3. Shrink central bureaucracy and let schools make more decisions.

4. Provide intense and sustained professional development to all staff.

5. Make sure all students are ready for school.

6. Provide students with the community supports and services they need to succeed in school.

7. Provide up-to-date technology and instructional materials.

8. Engage the public in shaping, understanding, supporting, and participating in school reform.

9. Ensure adequate resources and use them effectively.

10. Be prepared to address all these priorities together and for the long term—starting now.

In order to accomplish this overall reform, the Children Achieving vision advocates the development of a coherent set of policies that support the vision; the provision of high-quality mathematics education for each student; and excellent preparation, continuing education, and support for each mathematics teacher. To implement these policies, the vision also advocates the convergence of the usage of all resources that are designed for, or that reasonably could be used to support, mathematics education—fiscal, intellectual, material, curricular, and extracurricular—into a focused and unitary program to constantly upgrade, renew, and improve the educational program in mathematics for all students. Salary increases for the superintendent and cabinet will be dependent on the degree of advancement shown by the students.

In the 1995-96 school year the major accomplishments of the Children Achieving reform agenda included (1) the implementation of a new form of district organization, the grades K-12 feeder-pattern cluster; (2) the development of content standards, aligned with national standards, in English/language arts, mathematics, science (included one year earlier than originally planned because of the urban systemic initiative), and the arts; (3) the creation of support systems to assist schools—for example, funding for professional development, a teaching and learning network, and a family resource network; (4) the initial implementation of a new comprehensive, high-stakes assessment system tied to national standards, the Stanford Achievement Test-9; (5) the development of new structures within schools to foster change in governance and instruction, such as local school councils and small learning communities; and (6) the implementation of full-day kindergarten in all racially isolated elementary schools.

Accountability

Beginning in school year 1996–97, the School District of Philadelphia implemented a "professional responsibility system" that holds administrators and teachers accountable for the achievement of students. All principals received training in a new "discipline, rating, and dismissal of professional and temporary professional employees system" that focuses attention on standards-based instruction and assessment. The major component of the system is the School Performance Index, a summary of a school's test results (Stanford Achievement Test–9 scores) in reading, mathematics, and science; the promotion rate (in elementary and middle schools) or the persistence rate (in high schools); and student and staff attendance. The School Performance Index provides a measure of where the school is now (the baseline is the school year 1995–96) and lets the school district set targets every two years, which will bring every school to high levels of achievement in one student generation (twelve years). The twelve-year goal for every school is an index score of 95. It is important to understand that the school is compared against its own baseline performance and against national and local standards, not against other schools.

Although the first identification of schools in the five categories will not take place until the summer of 1998, in late September 1997 the district released its School Performance Index for the 1996–97 academic year to provide each school, its parents, and the public with a midpoint evaluation of districtwide and school-based achievement. The results show that neighborhood schools raised their scores in reading, mathematics, and science.

Each two-year cycle has its own performance target—a percentage of growth that will keep the district moving toward proficiency. To reach the proficient level, the district must improve student performance by 5.9 points in each two-year cycle for the next twelve years. To make the performance goal for each cycle, every school and the district as a whole must meet two requirements: (1) reach its performance target on the School Performance Index, and (2) move 10 percent of its most poorly performing students into a level that demonstrates a basic achievement of academic skills. A policy was also adopted to require a rigorous review of mathematics curriculum materials to ensure alignment with national and local standards and to ensure they are included in the district's databank of best programs and practices.

Social Services

Additional policies have been implemented in the 1997–98 school year to implement the Children Achieving agenda. The school district has established a family resource network in every cluster. This network is coordinated with the city's human and social services programs to provide linkage, support, and access to services for children and families. These networks support the development of resources to ensure that all students' physical, social, and economic requirements are addressed so that all students come to school ready and able to learn. Each of the twenty-two clusters has an equity coordinator to ensure that all students have access to the resources and supports necessary for success in school, including meeting the district's quality learning goals. Every cluster has a community school that is open to parents, students, and community members in the evenings and on weekends for tutoring, technology training and access, GED classes, and other supportive programs.

Learning and Instruction

On June 29, 1998 the Board of Education adopted new graduation and promotion supports and requirements for implementation from 1998 to 2003. Current graduation requirements are 21.5 credits as follows: 4 English, 3 mathematics, 3 science, 3 social studies, 1.5 health/physical education, 2 arts and humanities, and 5 electives. The credit hours for students graduating in June 2000 are the same but the credits must cover a course of study that prepares all students to meet the District standards, and to have the option of pursuing employment and/or higher education. These standards may be met through coursework and internships that involve completing traditional coursework or through coursework and internships that integrate different subjects. In addition, students must complete a project that involves more than one subject and demonstrates citizenship, problem solving, communication, school-to career, multicultural competencies, and requires strong writing skills. Effective for students graduating in June 2002: 23.5 graduation units—4 English, 4 mathematics, 4 science, 3 social studies, 2 world language, 1.5 health/physical education, 2 arts and humanities, 3 electives and one-sixth of the final credit will be based on citywide performance-based final examination in those subjects (grades 11 and 12). Similar increased requirements in mathematics and science are included for promotion from middle grades to high school and from elementary school to middle school.

Every school is in some stage of developing small learning communities of 200 to 500 students. Once these communities are formed, teachers within them have the opportunity to plan together and may develop more-flexible instructional schedules. By June 1997, every cluster had at least one elementary, one middle, and one high school with fully operating small learning communities. All schools will be reorganized into small learning communities by September 1998.

Philadelphia became the first city in the nation to add African American, Hispanic American, and Asian American multicultural open-ended and multiple-choice items to the SAT-9. All the items have been piloted and will be added to the test in 1998. The district will continue to disaggregate all assessment data to ensure that all racial and ethnic groups and both genders are being equitably addressed and supported.

Successful implementation of the Children Achieving agenda requires long-term planning and the collaboration of resources. The district has established performance goals in two-year cycles to align the strategic planning and budgeting process and has assembled a group of cabinet members and middle-level administrators to address the issues of implementation. A "coordination of efforts" meeting is held biweekly to ensure that policy implementation is done efficiently and in a manner that reflects the rationale and intentions that drive policy decisions.

Conclusion

The School District of Philadelphia has established one set of rigorous mathematics standards for all students—including those from low-income families, of racial and language minorities, and with disabilities—that incorporates both academic and real-world competencies. Performance-driven assessment and accountability systems are in place to help achieve the standard that all students can and will achieve at high levels. A professional development system has been implemented to enable every teacher, administrator, and staff member to develop the knowledge, skills, and behaviors to create learning settings that enable all students to demonstrate high levels of achievement. All policies, all planning, and all decisions at all levels support the proposition of high expectations for everyone.

Professional Development Strand

Summary of Breakout Sessions on Mathematics Professional Development for Teachers of African American Children

Five groups of conference participants met to discuss the focus of plans for the Benjamin Banneker Association based on the presentation of Marieta Harris. The discussion groups were led by Ben Dudley, Ronald Bradford, Dorothy Strong, Vera King, and Marie Jernigan. The participants agreed unanimously that the professional development of teachers is paramount to improving the mathematical learning of African American children. The concerns and recommendations from the groups focused on (1) the needs of African American children, (2) elements of effective professional development, (3) professional development model programs for teachers of African American children, and (4) the role of the Benjamin Banneker Association in the professional development of teachers.

Needs of African American Children

The participants concurred that before we look at professional development, we have to make sure that teachers understand the culture, customs, and traditions of their African American students. The participants' goal is to have teachers be knowledgeable about students' experiences in order to teach mathematics effectively. Participants also agreed that teachers must understand that African American students need to have environments that promote student-teacher discourse, are rich in interactions and mathematics content, varied in instructional strategies and techniques, culturally congruent in curriculum and approach, focused on instruction that develops analytical skills, and equitable in tasks and interactions with teachers in order to promote achievement and success in all students. Moreover, students should be active participants in the learning process. They should participate in creating tasks as a means of developing and exchanging vocabulary, applying "real world" examples, and using their environment in conjunction with their prac-

tical knowledge to demonstrate mathematical concepts. The key to teachers having the skills to deliver such instruction is a stronger, more focused professional development program.

Elements of Effective Professional Development Programs

Conference participants defined "professional development" as the *education* of teachers as opposed to the training of teachers because teachers who are trained often revert to their more familiar pedagogies when they return to the classroom. When professional development focuses on educating teachers, the emphasis shifts to transforming teachers' attitudes and opinions about teaching and learning. Teachers are more apt to change their classroom pedagogy if they are educated in the ways of more successful teaching. Professional development education (as opposed to training) allows teachers to construct meaningful instruction for their African American students, who are in turn better equipped to construct meaning for themselves. One group at the conference appropriately called it *constructive professional development*. Collectively, the groups described the focus of the content for this constructive professional development as including some or all of the following:

1. Reflection on practice

2. Rich mathematics content

3. Information on the implementaton of reform in practice and standards-based curricula

4. The exploration and celebration of African American culture

5. Culturally relevant pedagogy

69

6. Authentic contexts with connections between social issues and mathematics instruction, involvement of parents and community

7. The implementation of a caring environment in the class that will empower students to learn mathematics

One of the most important aspects of professional development is that it must model the instruction that is desired from teachers in the classroom.

Model Programs

For guidance in establishing effective professional development programs that would include the aforementioned topics, the participants looked to established programs that have had success in these areas. Groups reported a need to look at successful professional development programs for teachers as models for effective professional development. Some of the suggested programs to review included Efficacy, GESA, Urban Learner Framework, EQUALS, Equity Institute, and Saturday Academies. Participants voiced concern that school achievement data in conjunction with potential success of professional development programs direct the development of professional development programs for teachers of African American children.

Role of the Association

Groups recommended that BBA be active in providing professional development opportunities for teachers and act as a "watchdog" to ensure that professional development programs address the needs of both African American children and their teachers. Participants want teachers of African American students to be prepared academically, fluent in pedagogies that address diverse learning styles and cognitive approaches to learning, and knowledgeable about how African history influences mathematics instruction. All groups agreed that BBA should write, publicize, and disseminate position statements concerning (1) professional development geared to the teaching and learning of African American students, (2) the quality of education offered to teachers of African American students, and (3) delivering good teaching to African American students.

In the area of programs, the groups recommended that BBA establish university partnerships with school systems to provide professional development, to develop educational components for teachers, and to offer staff development credits for school aides and assistant teachers. Also, they recommended the development of a general syllabus for mathematics instruction; the establishment of a center or clearinghouse for information on the teaching, learning, history, and culture of African Americans; and the compilation of a bibliography of information from databases on African American history, culture, programs, and other aspects, for publication.

In sum, the five groups that discussed Harris's presentation did much more than initial brainstorming. Taking professional development and its potential impact seriously, participants developed an improved vision for BBA—a vision that includes the professional nurturing of both African American students and the educators who facilitate their learning.

The Professional Development of Teachers of African American Students

Lee V. Stiff
North Carolina State University

Undoubtedly, the professional development of teachers of African American students consists of a set of knowledge, skills, and behaviors that are the same no matter who the prospective students may be. Knowing how to design instruction for student achievement, developing sound classroom management skills, and having positive expectations of student success are among the basic elements that define excellence in the professional development of all teachers (Wong and Wong 1991). However, professional development programs that attempt to address the needs of teachers of diverse student populations yet fail to take into consideration the teaching and learning preferences among different groups of students are destined to be ineffective. In this paper, I shall address some of the ways that strengthen the professional development of mathematics teachers whose prospective students are African American youth.

Designing Instruction for Student Achievement

Too often, we teach mathematics as we were taught. We must allow research in education to guide and enhance our teaching practices. Teaching practices born of our experiences as students can often be limited, particularly in mathematics. Those of us who pursued the study of mathematics may have flourished under traditional teaching practices, but we must remember that many of our classmates did not succeed or may have developed negative perceptions of mathematics and mathematics instruction. If we are to increase the numbers of students who do well in mathematics, then we must use sound teaching practices born of research in mathematics education to prepare teachers (see Jensen [1993], Owens [1993], and Wilson [1993]). Research in mathematics education should be complemented with research and readings about how African American students find success in school in general and in mathematics and science in particular (see Atwater, Radzik-Marsh, and Strutchens [1994]; Cuevas and Driscoll [1993]; and Trentacosta [1997]). Teachers of African American students must also conduct their own classroom research. Teaching practices, curriculum materials, and modes of assessment that promote success among African American students must become a focus of classroom instruction and assessment. Successful approaches can then be duplicated, monitored, analyzed, and disseminated, so that others can benefit.

One of the principal aspects of mathematics education reform is the emphasis on the teacher as facilitator. The focus of instruction should not be on mathematics teachers but rather on students. Effective instruction begins with the realization that students learn best when they are actively engaged in the process. Getting students to perform tasks, conduct investigations, do activities, or complete performance assessments are productive means for increasing their learning in the mathematics classroom. Stated differently, let students do the bulk of the work; let teachers monitor and support students in the process. For many teachers of African American students, making students responsible for the bulk of the work seems ill-advised. Often, teachers believe that control of African American students is paramount and can best be achieved in teacher-centered classrooms. But control is not the goal of classroom instruction, learning is. Teacher development programs must provide teachers with a greater understanding of the different ways people choose to learn, so that mathematics teachers may recognize that there are many different student behaviors that contribute to the learning process (Ladson-Billings 1997; Stiff and Harvey 1988; Trentacosta 1997).

Another important aspect of mathematics education reform is the attention given to the benefits of clear, concise, open communication of expectations of students' achievement.

That is, students' performance should be described in terms of observable behaviors that students create and develop throughout the learning process. Both teacher and students should be clear about what these behaviors are. Teachers must shift from telling students what to do to identifying what they should accomplish. This instructional modification can affect students' learning in subtle ways. For example, instead of making the assignment, "Do exercises 6 through 10," it is better to say, "In exercises 6 through 10, use the slope-intercept form of a linear equation to find the slope." Or instead of the assignment, "Read lesson 2.3 tonight," make the assignment, "Read lesson 2.3 tonight; be sure to identify and write down the terms that you do and do not understand." When both students and teacher can articulate what is to be accomplished in a lesson or a chapter, on a test, or during an activity, students' learning increases. Teachers of African American students must often develop a sensitivity and an awareness of whether the goals and objectives of instruction have been clearly communicated. Although each situation is unique, even if the prescriptions noted above have been followed, students may still misinterpret the intentions of an assignment, lesson, or evaluation. Certainly this is true for all students, but it is especially critical that teachers of African American students cultivate teacher-student exchange so that all parties concerned understand classroom interactions completely.

Similarly, student assessments should strictly reflect the stated objectives of the instruction. Student assessments should not contain surprises. Consequently, teachers need to share examples that represent the quality of work desired of the class. Examples of previous tests and the work of former students provide current students with useful information about reaching the goals established for the class. In this way, what is to be accomplished is made explicit in the work of other students. The alignment of instructional and assessment objectives further emphasizes the role of assessment as an effective tool for monitoring students' progress toward the established goals. For many students, especially African American students, assessments must be established as aids for learning. Often, students see assessments as unwelcome obligations to show what they cannot do. To prevent this perspective, teachers must take cues from past and current students about their preferred ways of demonstrating what they have accomplished during a lesson, chapter, or activity. If the connection between assessment and instruction is unbroken, then as African American students demonstrate what they know and how they know it, the improvement of instructional practices is immediate and ongoing.

Developing Sound Classroom Management Skills

Many mathematics teachers of African American students describe classroom management as their primary source of concern about instruction. Teacher development programs spend a great deal of time on developing classroom management skills. And, indeed, a well-managed classroom is easily spotted. In these classrooms, students know what is expected of them, class routines are well established, and students are at work in pleasant surroundings. In well-managed classrooms, teachers start class on time with clear and concise classroom assignments that get students working immediately. Behavior problems are few because teachers are prepared and ready for the lesson and students are working.

Teacher preparation, however, involves many different aspects of classroom instruction. Not only are instructional materials and equipment ready for students' use at the beginning of class, but the prepared teacher has planned the uses of floor space, wall space, and bookcases to promote student success. Furthermore, work areas, student areas, and teacher areas are designated within the classroom so that the teacher and students can meet their teaching and learning responsibilities efficiently and effectively in a pleasant work environment.

How should teachers of African American students approach classroom management? A few, perhaps less obvious, observations may provide some insight. As noted, floor space and wall space can be organized to promote sound classroom management. Desks should be arranged so that students can easily see the teacher at all times and the teacher can see them. The intent is to promote a personal connectedness between teacher and students. The arrangement should also provide a sense of community among all members of the class and promote quality interactions. This is especially beneficial to many African American students, who prefer to work cooperatively on class assignments and projects.

Wall space can be used to create a sense of belonging and achievement among African American students. Of course, bulletin boards should be used to prominently display classroom assignments, procedures, and the discipline plan. But wall space should also be used, for example, to display samples of students' work, birthdays of students and the teacher, and famous African American mathematicians and scientists of the past and present. In fact, students should be encouraged to conduct their own research on well-known African American mathematicians and scientists and give oral and written reports about them throughout the school year. Finally, examples of completed assignments that students will be assigned, tests that they will be given, and class projects that they will be asked to complete, should be posted on bulletin boards. Such examples will provide a sense of security for African American students because they will better understand what is expected of them.

Discipline plans and classroom routines promote pleasant work environments for students and teachers alike. Although there are many discipline plans that may be implemented, several principles of effective discipline are widely accepted: (*a*) students should be treated with respect, (*b*) good teaching and assessment practices eliminate many discipline problems, (c) academically successful students infrequently misbehave, and (d) students must be given some say about classroom rules. It is important that discipline plans not be confused with classroom routines. Routines are procedures that have become habits of behavior; procedures are the way we get things done in class. Unlike behaviors related to discipline, routines should have neither consequences nor rewards associated with them. Students must simply practice selected classroom procedures until they are done smoothly and automatically. Understanding the distinction between discipline problems and breaches in classroom routines can eliminate many unnecessary conflicts between teacher and students.

African American students frequently suffer penalties for failure to follow classroom procedures that have not been clearly articulated or carefully practiced because the teacher expects all students to share his or her sense of "appropriate classroom behavior." But, as previously noted, violations of classroom procedures are not discipline problems and should not result in penalties or rewards. Rather, procedures must be carefully explained, practiced, and reinforced until they become habits. Similarly, teachers often assume that classroom procedures need only be explained and that students' failure to comply represents a discipline problem. This is especially true for African American students, who may not regard a given set of procedures to be relevant or necessary because of varying perceptions of the classroom community and interpersonal relationships. If the teacher's and the students' perceptions of the classroom community and appropriate interpersonal give-and-take differ greatly, then avoidable confrontations may occur.

Allow African American students to enjoy academic success. Most discipline problems can be avoided by engaging students in classroom lessons, activities, and assessments in which they do well. From many students' perspective, it is better to behave badly in class than to be seen as "stupid." Careful attention to the knowledge, skills, and academic strengths students bring to a given lesson or chapter will help prevent needless failure and discipline problems. The lessons on how to design effective classroom instruction for student achievement become a powerful tool to reduce and eliminate discipline problems.

Finally, the ways many African American students prefer to interact in a social setting can be very different from what the teacher expects. Sensitivity to differences among all students will help teachers avoid placing negative interpretations on the classroom behaviors of African American students. Learning the variety of ways that African American students prefer to operate in their real-life environments, especially the school environment, is an important first step toward the understanding and appreciation of healthy human differences (Backler and Eakin 1993; Ladson-Billings 1997; Sleeter 1990).

Have Positive Expectations of Student Success

Students tend to live up to the expectations we have of them. These expectations can be positive or negative. Often, teachers have negative expectations of many African American students because they do not fit an image of success that has been often identified in the mathematics classroom. But as we have discussed, teachers affect students' success by the things they do in the classroom. A teacher development program can help prevent the establishment of negative stereotypes and create positive outlooks by exposing teachers to the wealth of successes among African American students at all levels of instruction (Cuevas and Driscoll 1993; Ladson-Billings 1997; Trentacosta 1997). Models of, and suggestions for, systemic schoolwide reform (Backler and Eakin 1993; Sleeter 1990; U.S. Department of Education 1986) should be identified and studied in teacher development programs. Clinical opportunities for preservice teachers to implement instructional strategies and approaches that result in successes in teaching African American students must be incorporated into teacher development programs. Without supervised interactions between prospective teachers and African American students, little insight and growth are likely to occur solely from readings and course study.

An important index of students' importance in the learning process and a subtle way to stress the value of success in the mathematics classroom spring from the way teachers dress for work. How we dress shows the extent to which we value our students and our role as teachers. Among African American students, appropriate dress on the part of teachers can achieve surprising results. Students are more respectful of appropriately dressed teachers. Well-dressed teachers gain wider acceptance from, and are viewed as more capable by, their students. Under these conditions, students are poised for success because a businesslike, success-oriented atmosphere has been established. Combined with well-designed lessons, a well-groomed teacher signals students that their success in mathematics is an important goal of the class.

African American students develop heightened interpersonal skills (Hale 1982). Many African American students are sensitive to very subtle behaviors on the part of their family, friends, and teachers. Teachers' genuine regard for students looms larger for most African American students than might otherwise be expected. Consequently, in the mathematics classroom, it is not instructionally effective to treat African American students in a professional manner while denying them an emotionally affirming environment. The value of caring for students can be found in raised expectations and strengthened support. Being respectful of African American students and extending unconditional love to them fuels their desire to return like sentiments. Mutual respect becomes the cornerstone of ambition and accomplishment. Positive expectations of students' success become the framework of their mathematical development. African American students learn to respect their own mathematical abilities because their teachers do.

References

Atwater, Mary M., Kelly Radzik-Marsh, and Marilyn Strutchens, eds. *Multicultural Education—Inclusion of All*. Athens, Ga.: University of Georgia, 1994.

Backler, Alan, and Sybil Eakin, eds. *Every Child Can Succeed: Readings for School Improvement*. Bloomington, Ind.: Agency for Instructional Technology, 1993.

Cuevas, Gilbert, and Mark Driscoll, eds. *Reaching All Students with Mathematics*. Reston, Va.: National Council of Teachers of Mathematics, 1993.

Hale, Janice. *Black Children—Their Roots, Culture, and Learning Styles*. Provo, Utah: Brigham Young University Press, 1982.

Jensen, Robert J., ed. *Research Ideas for the Classroom—Early Childhood Mathematics*. New York: Macmillan Publishing Co., 1993.

Ladson-Billings, Gloria. *Dream Keepers: Successful Teachers of African American Children*. San Francisco: Jossey-Bass, 1997

Owens, Douglas T., ed. *Research Ideas for the Classroom—Middle Grades Mathematics*. New York: Macmillan Publishing Co., 1993.

Sleeter, Christine E. "Staff Development for Desegregated Schooling." *Phi Delta Kappan* 72 (September 1990): 33–40.

Stiff, Lee V., and William B. Harvey. "On the Education of Black Children in Mathematics." *Journal of Black Studies* 19 (December 1988): 190–203.

Trentacosta, Janet, ed. *Multicultural and Gender Equity in the Mathematics Classroom—The Gift of Diversity*, 1997 Yearbook. Reston, Va.: National Council of Teachers of Mathematics, 1997.

U.S. Department of Education. *What Works—Research about Teaching and Learning*. Washington, D.C.: U.S. Department of Education, 1986.

Wilson, Patricia S., ed. *Research Ideas for the Classroom—High School Mathematics*. New York: Macmillan Publishing Co., 1993.

Wong, Harry K., and Rosemary Tripi Wong. *The First Days of School*. Sunnyvale, Calif.: Harry K. Wong Publications, 1991.

Closing

Conference Summary and Charge to the
Benjamin Banneker Association

Challenges in the Mathematics Education of African American Children

Edgar Edwards
Richmond, Virginia

The Benjamin Banneker Association (BBA) held this conference to encourage participants to think about the BBA goals and to use these goals to make plans for our future. We have discussed numerous questions in the three days of the conference. How do we encourage teachers to examine and decide whether or not they want to join the reform movement? How do we support teachers in the reform movement? Do the new curriculum materials represent a variety of cultures? How do we promote the belief that all children can learn? All of these are real challenges. Conference participants requested many things of the BBA, including a list of strategies to assist teachers in dealing with the battles that teachers fight each day. In all reform movements we place an enormous responsibility on teachers. Participants talked about how we must understand and deal with the effects of both elitist attitudes related to mathematics learning in our schools and institutions and attitudes about the deficits of African American students in mathematics. We discussed accountability, teacher certification, teacher assignment, and a number of other issues.

I do not intend to review every segment of this meeting because the conference was organized in such a way that everyone had an opportunity to provide input about each of the sessions through the break-out group meetings. This process is exceedingly important to the future plans for our association. It would be redundant for me to reiterate our discussions; therefore, I will summarize what I believe are the major points of our discussions and make a few recommendations. These points and recommendations indicate the depth and breadth of the task before the Benjamin Banneker Association and offer suggestions for our next steps.

1. That an ad hoc task force be appointed to study the proceedings of this conference and that the findings be used to assist the BBA board in deciding on areas of focus

The board needs to look at the conference and proposed recommendations and decide on our focus. This task force will be able to provide the board with the necessary help in identifying and prioritizing our association's focus—its future positions and actions—based on this conference.

2. That participants of this conference make a conscious effort to seek out and inform the association of local and national situations where BBA's involvement may make a difference

The only way BBA will know what is going on across the United States and Canada is if members stay in contact with the board and fellow members. BBA leaders are aware of the issues we are discussing here at this conference, but they may not be knowledgeable about situations in your specific localities. You need to inform the board if and when there are situations where BBA's influence is needed or where it can provide guidance and support.

3. That the board develop a set of guidelines for selected mathematics instructional materials and distribute them to the membership

During the conference, participants have examined curriculum materials developed by National Science Foundation–supported projects and Creative Publications. We have a lot of questions regarding curriculum materials. How do we know what is most appropriate for African American students? How do we know whether or not materials are in keeping with the NCTM *Standards*? How do we know they are in keeping with the reform movement? If the board can develop guidelines and distribute them to the membership, this will help those individuals who are looking at instructional materials. Some individuals come from states where textbook adoption takes place at the state level. Others come from states where textbook adoption is done locally. In both situations BBA's expertise can contribute to, and guide, these decisions.

4. That BBA form a task force to study and identify the kind of problems and concerns related to educational policies that have the potential to affect African American children or teachers

This recommendation is a difficult one. Local, state, and national policies sometimes create many problems for the education of African American students in mathematics and at other times they are helpful in the education of African American students in mathematics. In one of the conference sessions, we learned of a number of policies that are helping students in Philadelphia. But sometimes policies create problems—our propensity to use testing as an accountability measure is one example. A number of states are now mandating tests, and a number of states are also mandating course tests for graduation. In fact, I think the state of Virginia is planning to mandate approximately nine end-of-year tests.

We are aware that some groups of students do not score as well on tests as others, but we continue to try to work with these students and help them be successful. Expansion of testing programs to the point where students are tested almost every year will make it difficult for many students, especially African Americans. I was reading something the other day about a legislator who said that he grew up on a cattle farm and to him, "you don't fatten your cattle by weighing them but by feeding them." We all know that improved teaching does not increase through an increase of testing. However improvements in instructional programs are needed.

5. That the board seek funds to hold a leadership conference, similar to this conference, in each BBA region

This recommendation matches one of the goals of this conference, and we have been working in our regional caucuses at this meeting to plan these conferences. It is imperative that we work actively to ensure that these conferences bring pertinent information and energy to our membership in all our regions.

6. That BBA use the good influence of its professional status to encourage institutions of higher education to strengthen preservice education for aspiring teachers by using practices identified by the reform movement

I think we have much to do in the area of staff development for practicing teachers and helping teacher training institutions become exemplary in preparing teachers of mathematics, especially in how to teach African American students. We have a number of college people in the organization, and we think that you can be proactive in this area.

One area that we did not discuss as much as I would have liked is program evaluation and how we can help teachers to develop such skills—how we can help teachers learn to collect and use data. Teachers must be able to recognize good and exemplary programs in mathematics and be able to determine whether or not a program is appropriate. Very often we look at the practice, but we should also examine the effects of a program.

Another issue that was originally not on the conference program but was included because of recent national initiatives is standardized testing in mathematics. I am not sure what role BBA should take in this national testing program, but I am sure that we must discuss the issue and formulate a unified position.

When Howard Johnson introduced the speaker on the opening night of the conference, he said we had a good conference on the agenda. After three days of meetings, including general sessions, breakout sessions, small-group discussions, and brainstorming sessions, we realize that the conference planners have done an outstanding job. We were fortunate to have had speakers who were well informed in contemporary mathematical thinking and also aware of the challenges in providing mathematics education for African American children. It is paramount that the ideas advanced at this conference be used to promote an agenda for the improvement of mathematics education for all children.

Epilogue

Future Plans of
the Benjamin Banneker Association

Carol E. Malloy
University of North Carolina at Chapel Hill

The Benjamin Banneker Association is very pleased with the results of this leadership conference. We are equally pleased and excited about the level of enthusiasm participants had in identifying issues and questions that the conference should address, in discussing these issues in both formal and informal conversations, and in making plans and creating programs in the six BBA regions.

The conference was initiated to promote conversations about teaching and learning, policy, professional development, and reform related to African American children's learning of mathematics. Through the application process, the participants extended the conversations of the conference to questions regarding issues of racism, power, and society and their relationship to African American children's mathematics learning.

Using the wealth of material and information that came out of the conference, the Benjamin Banneker Association is now able to implement plans for the future. We are prepared to be more visible on the national level. We are prepared to celebrate the achievement of African American children and their teachers in national as well as local forums. We are prepared to address major issues that affect the teaching and learning of African American children through our participation in national and local meetings, our participation on boards where policies are made, the development of professional development materials, and especially in the distribution of BBA position statements on the education of African American children. We are prepared to meet the challenge of educating African American children in mathematics.

We thank all the participants for contributing their ideas and experiences to this important event, and we warmly acknowledge their expertise, dedication, and passion about the mathematics education of African American children.

Conference Participants

NAME/POSITION/CITY/EMAIL	REGION	NAME/POSITION/CITY/EMAIL	REGION
Bennie Adams Community College Florissant, MO	SC	Alverna Champion NSF Arlington, VA achampio@nsf.gov	SE
John (Jack) Alexander NAM, President Atlanta, GA	ORG	Michaele Chappell University Temple Terrace, FL chappell@tempest.coedu.usf.edu	SE
Phyllis Arnette Texas Instruments Princeton, NJ parnette@TI.com	NE	Vanessa Cleaver Math Coordinator Little Rock, AR vecleav@lrsdadm.ersd.k12.ar.us	SC
Suzanne Austin Community College Miami, FL saustin@kendall.mdcc.edu	SE	Duane Cooper NCTM-CME College Park, MD dac@math.umd.edu	SE
Jennie Bennett Administrator Houston, TX JenBenn@tenet.edu	SW	Steven Cox University Administrator Philadelphia, PA	NE
Barbara Berman Consultant Staten Island, NY	NE	Margaret Cozzens NSF Arlington, VA mcozzens@nsf.gov	ORG
Gwendolyn Bradford Teacher Houston, TX	SW	Ella Mae Daniel Teacher St. Croix, VI	SE
Ronald Bradford Administrator Richmond, VA Rock2@Erols.com	SE	Frank Davis Lesley College Cambridge, MA fdavis@lesley.edu	NE
Sybil Brown Teacher Columbus, OH Brown.109@osu.edu	NE	Arnitra Duckett Texas Instruments Temple Hill, MD aduckett@ti.com	SE
Gail Burrill NCTM, Past President Hales Corners, WI gburrill@macc.wisc.edu	ORG	Paula Duckett Washington DC Public Schools Temple Hill, MD pduckett@nsf.gov	SE
Patricia Campbell University College Park, MD pc2@umail.umd.edu	SE		

NAME/POSITION/CITY/E-MAIL	REGION	NAME/POSITION/CITY/E-MAIL	REGION
Benjamin Dudley Consultant Willingboro, NJ	NE	Gary, IN mjern16403@aol.com	
Edgar Edwards, Jr. Consultant Richmond, VA	SE	Howard Johnson University Syracuse, NY hjohnson@suadmin.syr.edu	NE
Dennis Estrada Creative Publications San Francisco, CA destrada@tribune.com	W	Arneita Jolly Teacher Cleveland, OH	NC
William Fitzgerald University East Lansing, MI	NC	Doyt Jones Teacher Philadelphia, PA dojones@phila.k12.pa.us	NE
Linda Fulmore Administrator Cave Creek, AZ lfulmo@phoenix.usd.k12.az.us	SW	Jacqueline Joyner Administrator Richmond, VA	SE
Linda Hall Administrator Tulsa, OK lhall@galstar.com	SW	William Joyner Principal Richmond, VA wjoyner@pen.k12.va.us	SE
Oretha Hargro Program Coordinator Vacaville, CA Ohargro@uclink4.berkeley.edu	W	Patricia Kenschaft University Upper Montclair, NJ kenschaft@math.monclair.edu	NE
Carol Harris Teacher Houston, TX	SW	Vera King University Houston, TX vera_king@pvamu.edu	SW
Marieta W. Harris Administrator Memphis, TN mharris451@aol.com	SC	Genevieve Knight University Columbia, MD gmk01@juno.com	NE
Harriet Haynes Administrator Brooklyn, NY	SC	Gloria Ladson-Billings University Madison, WI billings@macc.wisc.edu	NC
Gilda M. Hester State Department St. Louis, MO	SC	Glenda Lappan University East Lansing, MI glappan@math.msu.edu	NC
Idorenyin Jamar University Pittsburgh, PA jamart@pitt.edu	NE	Gwendolyn Long Principal Chicago, IL lizmath@aol.com	NC
Marie Jernigan Administrator	NC	Linda Love State Department	SE

NAME/POSITION/CITY/EMAIL	REGION	NAME/POSITION/CITY/EMAIL	REGION
Raleigh, NC llove@dpi.state.nc.us		University Raleigh, NC lee@poe.coe.ncsu.edu	
Beatrice Lumpkin Consultant Chicago, IL bealumpkin@aol.com	NC	Dorothy Strong Consultant Olympia Fields, IL dorothysse@aol.com	NC
Carol Malloy University Durham, NC cmalloy@email.unc.edu	SE	Mary Thomas Teacher New Orleans, LA mthomas1@communique.net	SC
Desiree Manuel Assistant Principal San Diego, CA desireemanuel@sdcs.k12.ca.us	W	Donald Thompson Teacher Florissant, MO dthompson@dtdl.slps.k12.mo.us	SC
Barbara Marshall Teacher Sicklerville, NJ bmarsh3363@aol.com	NE	Clara Tolbert Administrator Blue Bell, PA ctolbert@sdp2.philsch.k12.pa.us	NE
Terri Moore Teacher Creve Coeur, MO terpiano@aol.com	SC	Agnes Tuska University Fresno, CA agnes@math.csufresno.edu	W
Reginald Obiamalu Administrator Torrance, CA amalu@aol.com	W	Fred Uy NCTM-CME Bayside, NY fuy@unis.org	NE
Irene T. Outlaw Administrator San Diego, CA outlaw@sdcc14.ucsd.edu	W	Irvin E. Vance University East Lansing, MI vance@math.msu.edu	NC
Andrea Prejean University Washington, DC aprejean@american.edu	SE	Bonnie Walker NCSM, President Houston, TX bkwalker@tenet.edu	ORG
Hazel Russell Teacher Fort Worth, TX	SW	Barbara Wells University Administrator Los Angeles, CA bgwells@ucla.edu	W
Anthony Scott Principal Chicago, IL ascott@teacher.depaul.edu	NC		
Mary Ann Sherman Teacher Gary, IN sherman@netnitco.net	NC		
Lee V. Stiff	SE		